Reactions to Notes from an even Smaller Island

"Hilarious, controversial, honest, revealing and most candid."

– Perut Buncit

"Siaow Kah Peng! If sit on MRT or bus, sure laugh loud loud one!"

– Derrick Tan Ah Beng

"What a disgrace! As a secondary school teacher, I find this book an insult to the intellect of the average Singaporean."

– Mrs Lek

"This book – can, ah. I like, I like! Can see myself in it, lor."

– Candy Lim Ah Lian

"Neil Humphreys is a rare breed. Comical episodes seem to follow him wherever he travels. Whether it be growing up in working-class England or living in middle-class Singapore, he always seems to meet the weird and the wonderful."

– Charles Smythe

"Very good, what! The tr

What the media said about
Notes from an even Smaller Island

"He pokes fun at Singaporeans... but rather than bristle at his observations, you are likely to twitch with mirth. The ribbing is always cushioned by good-natured quips often sprinkled with hilarious anecdotes."
— *The Sunday Times*

"The book presents a warts and all view of the city-state and celebrates many of the things most often criticised." — *BBC World*

"A candid look at the idiosyncrasies of Singapore and Singaporeans."
— *TODAY*

"It's a great insider's look at Singapore from an outsider's point of view."
— Malaysia's *Sunday Mail*

"Humphreys' laugh-a-minute self-deprecating manner makes this book very entertaining... No punches pulled. Bravo!"
— Malaysia's *Sunday Star*

"Humphreys' humourous take on Singapore is an entertaining read... It is hard not to smile while reading this book."
— *Woman's World*

"Blatant prejudices are chewed on, digested and spat out with an equal measure of candour and tongue-in-cheek."
— *Singapore Seventeen*

"A thoroughly enjoyable read on the virtues (or hazards) of living in Singapore through the eyes of a 6ft 4 inch Briton whose style is so disarmingly honest, you will laugh at the things you once considered the bane of your existence... Decidedly Singaporean, distinctly British."
— *Singapore FHM*

Notes from an even Smaller Island

Neil Humphreys

TIMES EDITIONS

Reprinted 2001, 2002, 2003, 2004

Published by Times Editions – Marshall Cavendish
An imprint of Marshall Cavendish International (Asia) Private Limited
A member of Times Publishing Limited
Times Centre, 1 New Industrial Road
Singapore 536196
Tel: (65) 6213 9288 Fax: (65) 6285 4871
E-mail: te@tpl.com.sg
Online Bookstore: http://www.timesone.com.sg/te

Malaysian Office:
Federal Publications Sdn Berhad (General & Reference Publishing) (3024-D)
Times Subang
Lot 46, Persiaran Teknologi Subang
Subang Hi-Tech Industrial Park
Batu Tiga, 40000 Shah Alam
Selangor Darul Ehsan, Malaysia
Tel: (603) 5635 2191 Fax: (603) 5635 2706
E-mail: cchong@tpg.com.my

National Library Board (Singapore)
Cataloguing in Publication Data
Humphreys, Neil
Notes from an even smaller island / Neil Humphreys. —Singapore : Times Editions, 2004.
p. cm.
ISBN : 981-232-797-5
1. Singapore — Anecdotes. I. Title.
DS609 959.57 — dc21 SLS2003036847

Printed in Singapore by Utopia Press Pte Ltd

Acknowledgements

Some people say that writing a book is a torturous experience and, my God, I would have to agree with them. However, there are many masochistic individuals who helped the process along with their support, encouragement and the occasional blow to the head.

I will always be grateful to my publisher for being brave enough to take a risk with this work when others would not. I would also like to thank my editor. There was a lot of blood, sweat and tears along the way but she just wiped them all off the manuscript and we carried on.

This book would not have been possible without my dear friend David, who brought me to Singapore in the first place, and Scott, my old travelling partner. David gave me a goddaughter, Scott gave me an excuse to swear a lot. I will always be grateful for both.

For inspiration, I must acknowledge the people of Singapore (and Dagenham!). I hope they will still speak to me after this.

The support of my wonderful family has been vital and I thank my mother for always being there and for being a 'real woman'.

But I dedicate this book to the one person who stood over my shoulder every day to remind me that my writing was utter crap.

This one is for my best mate, Tracy, for always being my best mate.

Prologue

There is nothing like being mugged twice to make you want to leave a country and head for a tiny equatorial island in Asia.

But that is exactly what happened.

The first time was farcical. When I was seventeen, a couple of friends and I were going to a nightclub called Fifth Avenue, which was full of young girls with too much make-up and pushed-up cleavages. Tacky, but teenage heaven. Naive and about as subtle as a kick in the head, we wore our Sunday best and all the jewellery we could lay our hands on and headed out. We looked like a mugger's pension scheme as we went into a hamburger place opposite the club.

Considering I was less streetwise than Harry Potter back then, it did not register that the only people in the restaurant were a gang of youths standing near the counter. We strolled up to the counter, waving £10 notes and jangling jewellery like a pawnbroker.

A boy came up to me and asked if I could give him fifty pence. Alarm bells were not yet ringing, as the young lad looked as if he had only just moved onto solids. Momentarily stunned, he hit me with a line that now seems spectacularly hilarious.

'Come on,' he said, 'give me fifty pence or I'll kill you.'

'What?' I asked in disbelief, still failing to take this surreal situation seriously. Then he sat down next to us and magically produced a knife. Surely this was not happening. Ironically, a police patrol car was parked directly outside the front of the restaurant.

'Now, don't fuck about. Give me fifty pence now,' my new companion continued.

Then I audaciously attempted a ploy that still tickles me. I haggled.

'How about I give you thirty pence?'

'I want fucking fifty.'

'Look mate, I'll give you thirty as I need to get the bus home.' I still was not taking my eleven-year-old mugger seriously.

'Those blokes over there are all with me and they're watching me, so don't fuck me off.'

This revelation unequivocally altered the odds. There were between eight and ten guys standing just behind the boy, monitoring his 'progress'. I strongly suspect their young protégé lost his cherry with us. What else could we do? They were all in their early twenties and looked like they should be playing basketball in the NBA.

I lost thirty pence but my other friend, who naively opened his wallet in front of the apprentice mugger, was relieved of £10 and a watch. We hurriedly left the restaurant, walked past the oblivious policemen parked outside and dejectedly went home. My deteriorating view of law and order in Britain took another downward turn. Surely there had to be a more suitable alternative to this?

Four years later, I found myself sitting in a stockbroker's office in

London earning obscene amounts of money. I had just graduated from the University of Manchester and needed money quickly as I intended to travel. I worked in the static-data department, yet, to this day, I still cannot fathom the value of what I did, what the purpose of my job was and who benefited from it. What did I do? Well, I took a set of figures from one computer column and transferred them to another. Then at the end of my first week working there, everything became clear. A payslip landed on my desk. It was my first since I had left university and I decided on the spot that I wanted to be a static-data man for the rest of my life.

As the numbers mounted on my in tray, so too did the figures in my bankbook. I had long entertained the prospect of exotic travel and now I had the wad of notes to do it. At university, I had met a man, as you do, called David. David was Chinese Singaporean and had invited me to stay with him in Singapore. My reply was 'sure', wondering where it was in China.

That is disgraceful, I hear you cry. Such geographical ignorance borne out of years of jingoistic sentiment. The sad fact is that you would be right. Large sections of the British population hold a rather simplistic view of geography and demography that has been cultivated by their educators – the tabloid media – for several decades and it goes like this. Decent white people come from Britain, loud white people come from Australia and loud, arrogant white people come from the United States. Darker white people with silly accents come from Europe, which is approximately fifty thousand miles away, and brown people come from Pakistan, a country that is quite good at cricket and its natives come to England to set up corner shops. Black people come from Africa, which is where Sir David Attenborough goes to make his wildlife programmes. Yellow-skinned people come from China, where they spend their days bowing and eating with chopsticks. China, by the way, is in the Far East, which is just off the coast of Mars and has something to do with communism. This, in turn, has something to do with a man called Lenin. Or is it Lennon? Something to do with the working classes, anyway. All of these 'foreigners', who, of course, cannot speak a word of the Queen's English (well, not proper English like what we do), come to England periodically to take everybody's jobs and claim social security benefits. Hell, it is enough to make you bang your chest, wave a Union Jack and sing *God Save the Queen* while standing on a silver jubilee tea tray.

However, I digress. As I was saying, I promised to visit my friend in Singapore while muttering to myself, 'I will visit your sacred land the day Lord Horatio Nelson gets his eye back and Gibraltar is returned to Spain.' I needed to be convinced further that my future lay on an island smaller than Greater London. I needed to be mugged again.

I am a diehard fan of the rock group Oasis. I know all about their childish arrogance and abhorrent attitudes but I just love their music. So when I heard that those belligerent brothers from Manchester were going to stage the two biggest gigs that Europe had ever seen at Knebworth in the summer of 1996, I knew I would be there.

On the eve of the gig, my friends and I had a little drink to celebrate the occasion. From what I remember, the night was a classic. Being friends with the landlord, we had 'afters', which meant we could drink into the small hours of the morning. Around 2 a.m., we reached the moral dilemma shared by pub drinkers everywhere to quote the famous Clash song: 'Should I stay or should I go now?' And the conversation, as always, went like this:

Sensible one: 'Drink up! We've got just enough money between us to get a taxi.'

Danny: 'Bollocks! I'm not going anywhere while there is still un-drunk Guinness left on the table.'

Most intoxicated one (me): 'What's all the fuss about? We're going to see Oasis tomorrow. Besides, it's your round Danny so sod off up the bar.'

Danny: 'Bollocks! I'm not going anywhere while there is still un-drunk Guinness left on the table.'

Me: (singing) '...And after all, you're my wonderwall.'

Sensible: 'I'm tired and you two have to be up in five hours for the gig.'

Me: 'Relax, we'll sleep on the train. Everything's fine. Danny get the drinks in.'

Danny: 'Bollocks! I'm not going anywhere while... shit, it's all gone. Right, I'm off to get a pint of Guinness. Who wants one?'

And so we stayed. To this day, though, I wish we had retained just a shred of common sense and taken a taxi. We had to walk three miles home and, as we clumsily climbed a fence into a dark local park to take a short cut, we were asking for trouble.

Public parks are a strange phenomenon in suburban England. During the day, they welcome senior citizens walking their dogs while children laugh as their wheezing fathers push them on the swings. When the parks close for the day, however, they transform themselves under the cover of darkness into a den of sleaze. A place used only by gangs, drug addicts and young teenagers so desperate to have sex that they are willing to suffer sub-zero temperatures and risk catching frostbite on the bum.

Into this illicit cauldron stumbled three young drunks, for whom the real London world of crime and violence had stopped existing about five pints ago. Their world was one of Lewis Carroll: a world of giggling and nonsensical language. It was always on a collision course with London's depressing reality. It was a red rag to a bull.

I heard some noises in the background that sounded like young boys fooling around. So, because I was drunk and because I am mentally subnormal when I am drunk, I shouted out 'fuck off'. The rustling sounds of bodies moving in the distance were swiftly followed by fast-moving footsteps. In that split second, I sobered up and realised I had done something seriously stupid.

The frustrating thing was that we almost made it. Danny and I ran like racing greyhounds and we had almost reached the park's gateway. I could see the streetlights and passing cars drawing closer, signs of life that would make a public kicking less likely. Then I heard the 'sensible one' scream. His scream stopped Danny and me dead in our tracks.

'Come back! Neil! Danny! Please come back!' he cried.

Danny and I looked at each other with a rational soberness that was instantaneous. Believe me, there is no medical potion in the world that sobers you up quicker than fear.

We turned and walked back with all the enthusiasm of a pallbearer. When the sensible one emerged from the darkness, the first thing I saw was the six-inch-long blade held to his throat, which, and I know this sounds terribly pretentious, actually reflected the moonlight. It was being held by a guy whose first impression immediately substantiated my belief in Darwinism. He was so stoned I could have got high from his breath. He was flanked by two morons who wielded neither a weapon nor a brain and were clearly the sheep in this operation.

The knife man wanted to know which one of us had shouted out 'fuck off'.

Nothing can accurately describe how I felt or how my body reacted. At that moment, I hated the world for all its bitter ironies. With plans to travel the world in the near future and on the very day I intended to see Oasis perform, I was going to either die or, at the very least, spend the rest of my life with a face resembling the London Underground map. There was only one thing to do: lie my arse off.

'I said it. I shouted it out to some blokes who were in front of us, giving us verbal. That's who we were chasing.'

'Don't lie to me. Don't fucking lie to me. Do you think I'm a cunt or something?' asked knife man. Answering this question truthfully would have really dropped us in it.

'Look mate,' I said, 'we don't want any aggravation. We don't want to fuck about. We're just on our way home.'

In a way, this put knife man in a difficult situation. He had only gone out that night to get stoned. He certainly did not want to commit first-degree murder. I mean, that could really spoil your weekend, couldn't it? He also had to contend with his two young protégés who were observing his every move. Knife man had to do something quickly.

'Give me all your money,' he said, delighted with his powers of improvisation.

We handed over our wallets like naughty kids in a playground. I also had to forfeit a gold ring and the sensible one had to hand over his watch before he was released and we were sent on our way. We called the police, who knew we were drunk and refused to take us seriously. But at least we realised that the world's most intelligent thieves had made off with the princely sum of fifty pence. Clearly not enough to pay their annual subscriptions to Mensa. So that cheered us up a bit.

Meanwhile, my dear friend David sent me a letter kindly informing me that if I still intended to travel, there would always be a spare bed for me at his apartment.

With no hesitation whatsoever, I left for Singapore three months later.

My good friend Fran swears this story is true. He lives in Bukit Batok in the western part of Singapore and was late for work one day so he hailed a taxi. The taxi pulled over to the kerb and Fran got in. He was greeted by a middle-aged Chinese Singaporean in perpetual motion, suggesting that he might explode if he stopped moving. His English was a little broken and the brief exchange that followed will stay with me forever.

'Hallo, where you go?' began the taxi driver breezily enough.

'Somerset Road, please.'

'East Coast, you go East Coast?' asked the taxi driver excitably.

The East Coast is a popular beach area among locals and tourists. I like the place but it is nowhere near Somerset Road, which is in the centre of town. In Singaporean terms, where you can be just about anywhere in 20 minutes, it is a million light years away from the East Coast.

'No, thank you,' continued Fran, 'I want to go to Somerset Road.'

'Yeah loh, East Coast, very nice. East Coast very pretty, what.'

'No. I would like to go to Somerset Road, please.'

'Oh... don't want East Coast?'

'No.'

'But East Coast nice. You go East Coast.'

'Somerset Road, please.'

'Yah, East Coast, you go East Coast.' The taxi driver was now having difficulty containing his excitement.

'Look, Somerset Road, I have to go to Somerset Road,' said Fran impatiently.

'East Coast, nice place, what.'

'Oh, fuck it.' With that, my friend bid the near-hysterical man a fond farewell, strangled him and hunted for a saner taxi driver, which is by no means an easy task.

What is the point of mentioning this alongside my two muggings? Well, I believe that each incident provides a neat microcosm of both England and Singapore, or at least they do for me. Of course, not everybody who lives in or visits England will become a mugging victim and not every cab driver in Singapore is half-demented but it goes much further than that.

England had and continues to have a vibrant arts scene that I, as a young Englishman, miss terribly. I could give a million reasons why Oasis will never play in Singapore. All of them, like fans needing to get permission to stand up and dance, would be depressing. I miss having a few beers with friends without having to mortgage my house first and, most of all, I miss the country's piss-taking sense of humour.

Nevertheless, Singapore gives me the one thing that I now cherish more than anything else – safety. Before people start thinking 'Oh, here we go again', I am not about to preach about the virtues of law and order. I agree that Singapore still has a long way to go in many respects and there are things about both the country and its people that drive me to distraction but I do feel that people here take their well-being for granted. Just think about those English and Singaporean incidents. The first gives an indication of the exciting freedom that a youth in England can have and the hedonism that money can buy. Make no mistake, sex, drugs and rock 'n' roll were readily available to me as a teenager and pursuing all three can be great fun. It is not a big deal. However, following that path almost culminated in one of my friends being carved up by a drug addict. That is a big deal.

That is why I prefer the Singaporean story. In essence, it is irritating, impatient and, to some, may even be downright annoying but it is also quite humorous and, most importantly, comparatively harmless. This is how I view Singapore right now. I know that I will return to England because I miss my family but for me, right here, right now, this city-state in Southeast Asia is a wonderful place to be.

Chapter One

In Singapore, a food court is called a hawker centre and I did not experience one on my very first night in the country. After a twenty-hour journey, I had arrived with my good friend Scott, a promising young architect from Yorkshire, at Changi Airport earlier in the day. Now anyone who lands at Changi Airport and fails to be impressed is either a liar or Helen Keller. It is a staggering example of what modern architecture and human efficiency can achieve. For those seeking a contrast, visit Malaga Airport in Spain and, after fighting your way through loud, sunburnt British families in matching shell suits, take a casual look around. Be enthralled by the countless non air-conditioned buildings, the sweaty armpits and the delayed flights. Then return to Changi. You will consider it no longer an airport but a Mecca for seasoned travellers. Enjoy the pleasurable sensation when you are struck with an irrepressible desire to bend down and kiss the spotless carpets. Although I attempted to do just this, I was promptly told to get up by a police officer wielding a very large gun. I tried to explain the whole Mecca thing but I could tell he was not really interested.

Anyway, Scott and I waltzed through customs (that raised a few eyebrows) and then we met David. Lots of embracing followed before we stepped out into the November sunshine. Thwack! Unlike Greece or Egypt, where the heat gently strolls up and tickles you under the arms, the Singaporean humidity positively head-butts you. Scott was raining sweat and I was seriously blushing. In fact, things could have got pretty tricky if we had not removed our coats and scarves when we did.

On the way to his car, David said, 'Did you bring umbrellas? There's going to be heavy rain today.'

I could not see a single cloud in the stunningly clear blue sky. 'Good one, Dave,' I said, 'you're still as funny as a migraine.'

Five minutes into the journey and I thought we had got caught in the middle of a marble throwing tournament. I cannot say that it started to rain because it did not. It just rained. Sun. Rain. Sun. Then rain again. Welcome to the Singaporean monsoon season.

Like the impending visit of the Inland Revenue, there is no warning. It just happens. Clouds appear, the deluge hits you and you are left wondering for the one thousandth time how those old women living along your corridor instinctively know when to bring in their washing. Then, just as you have manoeuvred your life raft into position, the Sun comes out, the miraculous drainage system has cleared the water and you are left looking a fool in the middle of Orchard Road holding a pair of oars.

We reached David's apartment in Toa Payoh, which is in central Singapore, shortly after. When he dropped off our two jet-lagged bodies into his apartment, he said there was a hawker centre opposite the apartment block if we got peckish.

Speaking to us as if we were mentally ill, David explained that a hawker centre is essentially a food court that contains a series of food stalls, each specialising in an Asian culinary delight. We simply go in, sit at one of the tables and wait for the person selling drinks to take our drink order. We then go to a stall, tell the hawker seller what we want and then retake our seats. Now what could be easier? At around 11 p.m., two tired young Englishmen set off on their first Asian adventure.

Following David's instructions, we crossed the road and spotted lots of tables with matching chairs. People were sitting around these tables eating various dishes and talking quietly: so far so good. With a boyish eagerness, we found an empty table, sat down and waited for the drinks seller to come round. Time passed and we noticed that we were attracting some strange looks. I would not say that these looks were aggressive but rather shocked and puzzled. I assumed it was because we were in the heart of the Toa Payoh community, one of the oldest housing estates in Singapore. It is not every day that two Caucasians, one standing at 6 feet, 4 inches and the other just over five feet, walk into a hawker centre.

After about five minutes, the staring had intensified and the drinks seller still had not appeared. Suddenly, Scott, who is not usually known for his eloquence, exclaimed, 'Fucking hell! There's a fucking dead body over there.'

'Where?'

'There! Fucking there. The one who is lying down and not fucking breathing.'

'Oh, shit. What are we going to do?'

'Well, I'm not fucking staying here if that's what the food does to you.'

We stood up with an indescribable sense of urgency, leaving our numerous observers open-mouthed, and fled the scene wondering what the hell went on in this bizarre country. I mean, I have eaten at places where you pick out the fish you want before it is cooked but this was something else. Had we inadvertently stumbled upon some satanic cannibalistic ceremony, where 'dishes' were carefully displayed and chosen? Were we to be the next course on the menu à la steamed 'ang moh'?

Of course not. We had simply walked into a funeral ceremony. If anyone who knew the deceased remembers two crazy jet-lagged white men treating the funeral service of their loved one like a restaurant, then I can only apologise. Having spent some time in the country, I now realise that funerals are often held at the bottom of apartment blocks in an area called the void deck. Should I now pass a funeral, I nod respectfully to those in attendance. But you have to admit that those wooden tables and red chairs are remarkably similar to the ones used in hawker centres.

We ended up having instant noodles before collapsing into bed where we proceeded not to sleep for almost six hours. The room had no air-conditioning so two exhausted Englishman, who had left brisk November temperatures of around 5–10°C, tried unsuccessfully to ignore the sweltering humidity and were forced to watch the Asian Sun rise.

We had heard about the ferocity of the local mosquitoes but being on the thirteenth floor, we had assumed that unless the flying pests were armed with rocket packs, we would be beyond their reach. We could not have been more wrong. Looking in the mirror the next day, we looked like we had spent a night in the village of the damned. The pulsating bites on Scott's legs were so big that he had to go to the doctor for fear of having one of his calf muscles burst.

As our flesh began to resemble a plate of beans on toast, I asked David out of desperation what we could do.

'Nothing,' he laughed, 'they only bite tourists.'

I have since concluded that he is right. I am not a doctor but I am sure that your immune system builds up some sort of defence to the 'mossies' as I seldom get bitten now. I have trekked through Bukit Timah Nature Reserve and I have cycled around the rustic island of Pulau Ubin. Each time, I have returned without so much as a peck on the cheek from our flying bloodsucking friends. So if you visit a new country and you spot one heading for the jugular, sing that country's national anthem or greet the mosquito in the local language. This should confuse and disorientate him and he will fly off in search of a new tourist.

Thankfully, though, my first impressions of Singapore went beyond the psychological habits of the mosquito and I soon detected a trend that enabled me to make a profound observation: size does matter. In everything. Everywhere.

Genetically speaking, Asians are not as tall as Westerners. Men are usually short and stocky while women are shorter and more petite. Of course, these are very general descriptions. Singapore has a population that is rapidly racing past four million. The Chinese, at 77 per cent, make up the majority while 14 per cent are Malay and just over 7 per cent are Indian. Foreign workers, like myself, make up the rest. Hence, it would be ignorant to suggest that the average Singaporean is of a certain height or build. However, it would be fair to say that I have yet to meet a Singaporean who is just over 1.92 metres tall, long-legged and has size 12 feet. Yet that figure stands before me in the mirror every morning. It also followed a dear old Chinese lady into a lift on the ground floor of an apartment block in Toa Payoh one afternoon. She looked at me, muttered something in Chinese and got out of the lift as fast as her little legs could carry her. The lift was still on the ground floor. I wanted to chase after her and say that I had just moved in but I figured that a lanky Caucasian chasing after a little old Chinese lady in flip-flops might cause a bit of a scene to passers-by.

Nevertheless, it must be said that if Singapore is guilty of any kind of 'ism', it has to be 'heightism'. I was once standing in a mini-mart, having a chat with the owners, when I felt a fly brush past my trouser leg. Thinking nothing of it, I swiped the fly away with my hand and carried on talking. Collecting my change, I felt the brushing sensation below my left knee again, only this time it felt more like a tug. I looked down to find the cutest little Chinese boy fiddling with my trouser leg with his right hand as he held his mother's hand with the other. He could have been no more than two years old but he had balls the size of watermelons. He made eye contact with me by craning his head so far back that it was almost at right angles with his spine. He then pointed up at me and bellowed in an astonishingly loud voice, 'Wah, so tall ah!' Looking exceedingly pleased with himself, he then started to giggle. I resisted the temptation to launch him into orbit with a swift dropkick and found myself laughing with him. His mother's red-faced apologies only made me laugh even more.

There was another incident in the same shop that not only shows the problems I have suffered with my height here but also demonstrates what a complete prat I am. I was once again being served and as I moved my arm suddenly to reach for my wallet I felt a dull thud against my right elbow, followed quickly by a distinct 'ooh' sound. Looking round, I saw a frail old Chinese woman rubbing her chin while repeatedly muttering 'ooh'. Quickly calculating her height and recalling the circular motion of my arm, I realised I had socked the poor woman on the jaw. I felt terrible. I mean it was an awful situation that was not helped when I spotted two schoolboys over her shoulder turning purple in their efforts not to explode with laughter. Anyone who has ever been in such a situation knows the predicament I was in. The episode was not without humour, to say the least, and laughter is contagious. Had those boys erupted (and the shopkeeper was not far behind), I would have followed and I know that laughing in the old dear's face would not have been the appropriate reaction. My precarious position was made worse by her apparent inability to say anything other than 'ooh'.

Biting my lip, I said, 'Auntie, I'm really, really sorry.'

'Ooh,' she replied, rubbing her chin.

'I don't know what to say. It was an accident.'

'Ooh,' came the reply once again.

The rubbing gathered momentum as the auntie adopted this endearing, puzzled expression that suggested she still was not quite sure what had happened. I wish I could lie but I had caught her squarely on the jaw and, to this day, I am amazed she remained on her feet. Eventually, she generously accepted my apology and I helped this wonderful woman, who was still 'oohing' and rubbing, out of the shop. If I am ever about to reach for my wallet now, I get the coastguard to conduct a thorough search first. I have also realised that laughing at old ladies who have been smacked on the jaw shows a complete lack of emotional intelligence. But, my God, it was funny.

It took me about a week to realise that Singapore does not cater for tall people at all. Admittedly because it does not have that many. When travelling on the Mass Rapid Transit (MRT) underground train system, the annoying handgrips that are suspended from the roof of each carriage have dealt me many a deft blow. On several occasions, I have had my pleasant daydreaming shattered by one of those stupid things smacking me on the back of the bloody head. Is it essential for these handles to wobble? It makes no difference to balance. I hold the fixed steel pole from which the handles hang and I have not fallen over yet. No, I believe the handles are deliberately made to be flexible by geeky engineers who thought it would be a titteringly-good idea to watch unsuspecting commuters get bludgeoned with them.

Additionally, I have no choice but to make a spectacle of myself every time I alight from a train. It is a real chore. When I am focused, I stoop slightly as the doors open so the sight of a tall, skinny hunchback greets everyone on the platform. That is fine. When, however, I am half-asleep, I get my head taken off by the low doorframe and it is extremely painful. That is most certainly not fine. When this happens, the doors open and those waiting on the platform are greeted by a lanky Caucasian rubbing his head and shouting, 'For fuck's sake!' Yes, it is that painful.

It does not stop there. Lift buttons, doorframes, rotating fan blades, off-the-peg clothing, shoes and urinals in public toilets – my height and build has caused problems in all these areas. In fact, ceiling fans are a particular nuisance.

My first job here was as a speech and drama teacher. At a pre-school one day, I was teaching a young class of toddlers the song "If you're happy and you know it, clap your hands". Noticing it was time to end the class, I sang, 'If you're happy and you know it, wave goodbye.' I then threw my hands up in the air. The rotating fan blades above swiftly brought them back down again. I was lucky enough to escape with a bad cut on my left hand. I thanked my lucky stars, though, because the kids enjoyed piggyback rides. The idea of receiving the death sentence for decapitating a pre-school child did not seem too appealing. I taught in that room for a year and no matter how much the sweat poured from the foreheads of those poor children, the fan was never switched on. The children might have lost a few kilos but they left the room in one piece.

To give an indication of the height and weight differences between me and the average Singaporean, I recently spent six hours scouring Orchard Road to find a collared shirt. I was not looking for a Ralph Lauren or a Hugo Boss but more of a Neil Humphreys, i.e., a shirt that fitted. There proved to be just one shop that had shirt sleeve lengths that matched my own. Consequently, I have devised a new shopping technique to save on the unnecessary preamble. On entering, I immediately ask the shop assistant to measure my arm length to see if they stock anything that matches it, usually something that Ah Meng, the orang-utan at Singapore Zoo, might have grown bored with. This process, save the assistant's giggling, takes about 30 seconds and I am soon sent on my way with the cry, 'Try Mr Frankenstein's tailors on the corner, you freak!' It may be humiliating but it does save time.

By the way, I do enjoy the frankness of the average Singaporean shop assistant. It is so refreshing. When I finally bought some shirts, I was delighted to find a shop that stocked clothes in my size in a variety of styles and colours. Usually, I get something along the lines of 'Yes, we do have one shirt that will fit you. I believe it was ordered by a Mr Cuthbert Nathaniel Smythe during those wildly excessive colonial days. This neon khaki safari shirt is a little dusty but I'm sure if I knock 10 per cent off, we'll say no more about it.'

So while I was paying for my purchases, I was eager to express my gratitude. 'I'm so glad to have found something that fits me. I've been looking for six hours.'

'That's because you're too long, lah,' said the young cashier who was folding my clothes.

'Am I?'

'Of course, what. You're so tall and your arms are really long. You'll never get clothes in Singapore.'

Fighting back the tears, I retorted, 'But I just have, haven't I?'

'Yeah lah, but only because we have European stocks and you've taken the biggest. I think you're too long for Singapore.'

'Oh, you don't fucking say.' Okay, I did not say the last part but I did collect my receipt in a rather hurried fashion. I also steadfastly refused to flirt with the young waif, even though I suspect she found me damned attractive with my ready wit and Neanderthal measurements.

Yet her in-your-face serving style is an example of one of my first impressions of Singapore. Its people can usually speak two or three languages and can write in at least two, an accomplishment that is extremely impressive to a man who is still struggling with his native tongue. How well each language is spoken depends, obviously, on age, education and socioeconomic background, all of which makes for some entertaining customer services.

When Scott and I began to eat in hawker centres, we found our early experiences terrifying. Men in black wellington boots would stand behind their respective stalls and if we ventured close enough would bellow, 'Wha' you want?' And when I say bellow, I mean bellow. This voice would slap you in the face and perforate your eardrums. Before you knew it, you were ordering things like boiled squid just so you would not get shouted at again. Then the woman who sold drinks would come to the table and take our order. She would never write anything down, yet she would go back to the drinks stall and collect the already waiting drinks. How did she do it? It is very simple. Female drink stall operators in Singapore have the loudest voices in the universe.

No matter which hawker centre you go to, the drinks seller will approach your table and eloquently ask, 'Want drink or not?'

To which you reply, 'Two cokes, please.'

Then it begins. She lifts her chin and points it towards the general direction of the drinks stall, which could be up to 25 metres away, with fifty talking customers in between. Opening her mouth to reveal a chasm that could easily fill Changi Airport, she stands up straight and, like Mount Vesuvius with a queasy tummy, erupts, 'T-W-O C-O-K-E-S, O-N-E C-O-F-F-E-E A-N-D T-W-O S-P-R-I-T-E.'

Scott and I jumped under the table the first time it happened. Never had I heard such a sound produced by a human being. Imagine standing on an airport runway as a Boeing 747 takes off, clearing your head by just a few metres. Think about the sound that those four engines make as they roar past. Now pretend they are saying 'Two cokes, one coffee and two sprite' and you will have some idea of what a female drinks seller in a hawker centre sounds like. Thirty seconds later, the same woman does it all over again, yet I have not come across a drinks seller who sounded hoarse.

Of course, I find hawker centres and their employees particularly endearing because I used to work in a café that was owned by my uncle in Bromley-by-Bow, an industrial area in East London. Our daily clientele consisted of enormous construction workers or lorry drivers, who used to grunt their orders, bitch about the prices and display their vast, greasy backsides while they ate. And I, a fourteen-year-old skinny teenager with zero confidence, was expected to serve them. No matter what I did, it was always wrong. How I used to wish that, for just one day, I was big enough to stand up to them and tell them all to fuck off. Now I wish I could have sent them 'hawker-centre woman'. Yes, sent 'hawkerwoman', the new crime fighter, to the heart of male-dominated, chauvinistic working-class East London to bring justice back to the world. Just one blast from her volcanic mouth would have scared the little shits witless. And should they have decided to pursue the matter, hawkerwoman would then have produced the chopper that the Hainanese chicken rice guy uses and decapitated each and every one of the bastards. Oh, you have got to have a dream.

One thing I have noticed since I have been here is the steady evolution from hawker centre to food court. Naturally, when friends visit from England, they extol the virtues of the bright, clean and efficient food courts. They remark that the food courts are much more hygienic than those grubby little hawker centres, which should all be swept away. I am not so sure. I have always believed that hawker centres do need radical face lifts. A country that strives for a knowledge-based economy could at least produce an eating establishment that was not littered with cigarette butts, used tissues and dropped food. However, without fail, hawker centres always produce good, cheap food. Food courts with their higher overheads cannot but, for whatever reason, they do not seem to be able to reproduce the quality of food produced in hawker centres either. If I am going to pay S$3.50 for a plate of chicken rice, then, at the very least, it must be as tasty as a S$2 plate from a hawker centre. But it is not.

So we are left, on the one hand, with modern food courts that are mediocre and overpriced and, on the other, hawker centres that still earn a small profit but not enough to undergo the essential renovations needed to compete in the new millennium. I just hope that when the sad day comes and the last hawker centre is swept away, I can still call upon hawkerwoman to save the day when I need her. Like I said, you have got to have a dream, haven't you?

Chapter 2

There is a song written by Robbie Williams called 'Millennium' that I believe could be an anthem for Singaporean 'aunties'. Whenever I hear the song, which contains the line 'Come and have a go, if you think you are hard enough', Singaporean aunties immediately spring to mind. To borrow from London terminology, I have yet to meet anyone who is 'harder' than a Singaporean auntie. Believe me, they are rock solid and their resolute attitude and lust for life is something that the younger, greedier generation can learn from.

A Singaporean auntie or uncle can be anyone who is from the older generations, like an English old age pensioner (OAP), and the term is used out of affection and respect. In a country where so much emphasis is placed upon the family unit and respecting your elders, it is only right that the elderly are held in such high esteem.

When the Japanese invaded and occupied Singapore, then a British Crown colony, in February 1942, these people endured terrible hardships. Under the constant surveillance of the *kempeitai* (the Japanese military police), many were imprisoned, tortured and even executed. Nevertheless, underground resistance groups still flourished until the war ended. When Singapore began its transformation from Crown colony to a leading Asian economic city-state, these hardworking people were the backbone. Far be it from me to deny the importance of the political direction of the Lee Kuan Yew-led People's Action Party to achieve prosperity but I am certain that modern-day Singapore owes everything to its aunties and uncles. So every time I see students and young executives brushing past them as if they were invisible to get on a bus or train, I really want to throttle the impatient little bastards.

Unfortunately, the same attitude exists in Dagenham, my home town, only it is much worse. Dagenham is in Essex, the county to the east of London. Built in the 1920s to take families away from the overcrowded London slums, Dagenham became home to the world's largest public housing estate almost overnight. Covering just 4 square miles, the town has a population of 90,000. However, the residents who first occupied its red-bricked boxes and made it a more homely place to live are now treated with contempt. When they are not being mugged, Dagenham's elderly are often abused in the high street by little parasites who would not be there if it was not for them. It is rare to hear a teenager in Dagenham addressing an elderly stranger with a term as respectful as 'auntie' or 'uncle' whereas it is still commonplace in Singapore. You have to be devoid of all respect and compassion to look an auntie in the eye and forcibly steal her purse but it happens in my tiny home town all the time.

I would like to lighten the mood a little, if I may, and talk about the wonderful aunties and uncles who make up over 6.5 per cent of Singapore's population (well, the ones over 65 do). I love 'em. However, the first thing a foreigner seeking to make a good impression must do is calculate whether a person actually qualifies for auntie or uncle status. Whatever you do, do not make the near fatal mistake of assuming that anyone older than yourself automatically qualifies to be an auntie or uncle.

Let's stick with the ladies to demonstrate this point as they tend to be more vociferous. When I was a teacher, a well-to-do parent covered in jewellery approached me at the end of a lesson for an update on her child's progress.

I said, 'Yes, of course. Your boy is doing very well, auntie. His vowel sounds are much more distinct and...'

'Auntie?' she shrilled. 'Did you just call me auntie? How old do you think I am?'

Like a bullet in the brain, my dad's two pearls of wisdom hit me. Never wear white socks with trousers and never, ever try to guess a woman's age. I am particularly poor at this exceedingly dull game and usually end up saying something like 'Ooh, you must be about eleven', which only serves to irritate everybody.

'Well, I'm sorry. I didn't mean to...'

'You can't call me auntie. I'm not old. You can only call old women "auntie". If my mother was here, you could call her auntie.'

What a conversation this was turning out to be. First, she wanted me to 'guess that age in five', then she wanted me to play 'happy families'.

'I understand and I'm really sorry if I...'

'Do you know, I've never been called auntie before. I'm only thirty-three. I've got two children. He's my elder son and he's only seven. You must be really careful who you call auntie, especially if it's a woman.' I wanted to disagree and say that surely I must be more careful of calling someone auntie if it were a man, but I thought better of it.

'Just remember that it can be rude to call a young woman auntie. She might turn around and scold you.'

As opposed to the friendly little chitchat that we have just had, I thought.

I cannot understand why she was so upset apart from the fact that I had aged her by at least twenty years. She should have been flattered that I had grouped her with Singapore's elite A-team. It would be like someone in England mistaking me for a member of the SAS Commando Unit, which happens all the time actually. I would be chuffed and you would be, too. The Singaporean aunties and uncles are a unique breed and they know it.

I remember complaining about the heat while waiting for a number 238 feeder bus in Toa Payoh one day. When it arrived, I lumbered towards it only to realise it was a non air-conditioned bus. About to unleash another pitiful whine, I was stopped in my tracks by the sight of my first Singaporean auntie in action. Wearing a trademark auntie pyjama suit, she marched determinedly towards the bus. Now I am not one to exaggerate but she had fifteen shopping bags in each hand while carefully balancing a grandchild on each shoulder. Without missing a step, she waltzed past me (and it just so happened that I was at the front of the queue) and got on the bus. To my astonishment, the old woman, who must have been in her late sixties and barely 1.2 metres in height, then managed to produce her farecard and insert it into the machine without dropping a single bag or grandchild.

The adventures of an auntie on a bus do not stop there. Should you be close enough to hear two aunties chatting, which is basically anywhere on a bus, you are guaranteed an entertaining journey. You see, aunties cannot converse quietly. When I first travelled on a bus here, I thought the elderly were wired up to a PA system. They usually sit directly opposite each other on the seats that face one another at the front of the bus and natter away.

I remember two wonderful aunties involved in an animated conversation on the number 54 bus. It was packed and I was one of the many people who had to stand. Yet right in front of me were two seated aunties who had slipped their shoes off to put their feet up on the seat facing them. They were making more noise than a chain saw felling a tree. It was marvellous. The two women jabbered away in what I think was Hokkien, one of the many Chinese dialects, and when they laughed, they roared. No one told the aunties to keep it down and no one asked them to make room for others to sit down. They certainly did not offer anyone else a seat and why the hell should they?

I am not saying that the elderly in Singapore are rude because generally they are not. Nor am I saying that British pensioners are without character or humour because that too would be a gross exaggeration. My own grandmother has left me doubled up with laughter more times than I care to remember. She is now in her eighties but until recently she used to perform her unique brand of Hawaiian dancing for guests. Weighing in at over 200 lbs, she would wiggle her hips ever so slightly while nonchalantly flicking her fingers out to the side. If you listened carefully enough, you might just catch the word 'Hawaii' escape from her lips. Moreover, she also enjoyed showing my girlfriends that she could not only still do the can-can but could also 'show her bloomers (knickers) with the best of them'. And she did.

Basically, all I am suggesting is that Singaporean aunties and uncles 'have got balls' as the Mafia would say. They are both resilient and fearless.

Take the Chinese auntie who cooked at a private pre-school that I used to teach at. She is a real woman whom I admire very much. If she ever decided to keep a diary, I know I would enjoy it more than those written by Bridget Jones, that fictional neurotic middle-class prat who took the British literary world by storm. Auntie was a real woman. Even performing the most mundane of tasks like travelling to school showed how hard she really was. Needing to prepare the schoolchildren's breakfasts, auntie would arrive shortly before me on her husband's motorbike. Walking to school, I would hear their large motorbike bringing up the rear. Wearing matching white crash helmets, they would go roaring past like two giant table tennis balls. Carrying her customary ten shopping bags of meat, fish and vegetables, I never once saw auntie hold onto her husband, no matter how fast the bike was going. Yet without fail, she would always raise one of her bag-laden hands and wave enthusiastically, causing the bike to wobble on several occasions, which, in turn, caused the driver to shout expletives at his demented wife. It was quite wonderful.

The school grounds were set in one of the few remaining rural parts of Singapore. The area was also home to some of the republic's more exotic species of animals such as monitor lizards and black-spitting cobras. On one memorable occasion, an enterprising cobra had slipped into one of the classrooms to seek a little sanctuary from the damp rainy conditions outside. Unsurprisingly, it was not long before the class was full of screaming children and teachers. In fact, one of the teachers jumped onto the table and became quite hysterical. As the smoke cleared, auntie appeared in the doorway with her sleeves rolled up, holding a broom in one hand and a bucket in the other. After being told that the snake was behind one of the shelves, she sprung into action. Moving the shelves, she thrashed around like a crazed psychopath. Fortunately, for the snake at least, it slithered through a hole and into the garden. The police eventually arrived and captured it. It is not often you sympathise with a black-spitting cobra but, knowing what it was capable of and knowing what auntie was capable of, I did.

However, I am delighted to report that she is neither the exception nor the queen of Singaporean aunties. No, the queen of Singaporean aunties would have to be Saudita – the major inspiration for writing this book.

Saudita is an elderly Indian woman who weighs about 250 lbs and has a tongue filthier than a drunken sailor. She could speak three languages: Tamil, Malay and swear. This mountain of a woman could strike fear into any man, woman or child who dared to cross her path. And she was my live-in landlady, from whom I rented a room for a year. To be honest, I am surprised that I am still here to tell some of her tales.

In twelve months, she must have sworn at me in every language except English, which she hardly knew. Indeed, her lack of spoken English led to many surreal telephone calls. First of all, she could not pronounce my name properly. It was always 'Neeoooh' with the pitch rising dramatically on the 'ooh'. I would be sitting in my locked bedroom when I would hear her cry 'Neeoooh!' Seeing me walk towards the phone, she would merely grunt and point at the receiver. Every time I picked up the phone, I would hear giggling on the other end. It reached the point when friends would call just to hear her shout my name.

Being on the receiving end was an experience, too. I telephoned the house once to speak to my girlfriend and the conversation was just bizarre.

'Hello, it's Neil.'

'No,' replied Saudita.

'Hello?'

'Hello.'

'It's Neil here.'

'No house.'

'What?'

'Neeooh, no house.' The penny dropped.

'No, *I'm* Neil.'

'Neeooh, no house, no house,' she said impatiently.

'No, I'm Neil. It's me on the phone. I'm Neil.'

'Out. Neeoooh out. No house. Out.'

'I'm fucking Neil, you silly cow. Now will you please put my girlfriend on the line before I come home and kill you.' She hung up. I suppose I asked for it really but she was such hard work.

She once asked me to use the dimmer switch to turn down the lights in Indian. Understandably, I was fluffing her cushions, cleaning her windows, feeding the cat she never had and performing every possible household chore except the one she wanted. In the end, when she ran out of patience and I had run out of things to turn on and off, the woman moved from one side of the sofa to the other and turned down the lights herself. It would be generous of me to say that Saudita was somewhat lazy.

However, everything changed at the weekend. The apartment was cleaned, the shopping was done and Saudita changed her clothes. Yes, she changed them just once a week and how she did it was chilling. Standing at the kitchen sink, she would take off her shirt and bra and wash her hair and upper body without making any attempt to cover herself whatsoever. Now if there was one woman on the planet who had two gigantic reasons to conceal her chest, it was Saudita. Being a rather large woman in her sixties, her breasts came down like two sacks of potatoes. Without a care in the world, she would then take her newly washed shirt, lean out of the kitchen window and peg it to one of the washing poles that were outside, with her ample bosoms bouncing all over the place. That is not all. The apartment was on the eleventh floor and faced another block that could not have been more than 20 metres away. I used to imagine some little boy in the opposite block saying, 'Mummy, there's a woman over there hanging out her washing and she's got three heads.'

Like most apartment blocks in Singapore, Saudita's shower room faced onto the kitchen. After taking a shower one evening, I opened the door to be faced by my bare-breasted landlady making *roti prata*. Astonishingly, she made no attempt to cover herself and scolded me in Tamil for not being in the habit of walking around with my eyes closed. Not wishing to get a nipple in the eye, I made a sharp exit. It happened many times after that. She could be making a variety of sumptuous dishes, all of which would leave you salivating until you found yourself face to face with the bare-breasted woman and you would make an instant decision to never eat anything again. To this day, I cannot buy a bag of potatoes without thinking about Saudita's chest.

Despite her hard exterior, she was quite a caring woman. On a delightfully sunny Saturday afternoon, my partner hung some washing on the line and discovered two hours later that it had been saturated by some uncaring soul who had hung out a dripping wet duvet on the floor above. Of course, no one is saying that a duvet cannot be cleaned but there is an unofficial law of courtesy within the apartment blocks whereby you do not hang out something that is large and soaking wet if there is washing hanging below. Now, the woman above had broken that unwritten rule and Saudita did not stand for it. She stormed upstairs and convinced the guilty party, via some carefully selected Malay swear words, to bring in the duvet until our washing was dry. Consequently, the duvet was withdrawn to allow my sopping wet underwear to win the day.

However, it is important not to get carried away here. I do have a tendency to romanticise things that I am particularly fond of and the older generations would certainly fall into that category. Nobody is perfect and the older generation has faults like everyone else. For me, the worst one has to be dogma. Every individual is entitled to his or her opinions but not to the exclusion of everybody else's. Elderly Singaporeans remain doggedly loyal to their own culture, cuisines and customs but I sometimes wonder how appreciative they really are of those of other racial groups. Of course, the moral do-gooders will jump up at this point and cry 'racial harmony'. Well, a racially harmonious society is the ideal and the government is certainly bending over backwards with its recent Singapore-21 committee. Still, I am not convinced. Just scratch the surface and look beneath the rhetoric of government committees and grassroots banners to see that the elderly might tolerate other cultures and customs but they do not accept them. In a world of constant change, they are shackled stubbornly to the past.

In 1997, the infamous haze, caused by the forest fires in Indonesia, engulfed parts of Southeast Asia. Singapore was badly affected, with air pollution reaching unhealthy levels on several occasions. Without sounding overly dramatic, the haze was so thick that I recall the Sun being obscured for long periods. If you stayed out for too long, you stood the chance of getting a headache or feeling nauseous. Around November of that year, the haze seemed to peak with the daily Pollutant Standard Index (PSI) recording extremely hazardous levels of over 200. The sky looked like it stopped just above your head and resembled the pea soup days of London's smog in the fifties.

One day, I had no choice but to step out into the thick of the haze to go to the mini-mart. On the way, I saw an elderly Chinese guy performing a common Singaporean custom under his apartment block. He was burning paper money in a large dustbin in the belief that the money will reach deceased friends and family members. This is usually done during the hungry ghosts festival or after a funeral. Without getting into a pointless debate about the actual merits of such ancient customs (not to mention their appeal to greed with people actually burning paper houses and cars in the hope that they will be waiting for them in the afterlife), it was his timing that irritated me. There we were standing in smog that was so thick that it reduced visibility to around 25 metres and he was trying to recreate the 1933 Reichstag fire. Perhaps that explains why I turned into Adolf Hitler.

'Do you have to do that now?' I enquired, just a tad irritably.

'Huh?' he replied, looking puzzled because, I suspect, he had not understood a word I had just said.

'Look at the sky. It's dark and gloomy and it's only 3 o'clock. So why do you have to do that now? Can't you at least wait until the air is slightly less poisoned? I mean, is it that important that you burn all that paper now? Can't you see the thick black smoke you are causing?' I continued to bombard the old man with questions but to no avail. He merely cursed me under his breath and went about his business of trying to turn all his dead relatives into millionaires while children still living on this Earth could not play outside because of the poor air quality.

On these occasions, I do become somewhat miffed at the elderly's stubbornness. It is also one of the few times that the government is powerless to react. Apart from grassroots committees putting up posters in apartment blocks asking residents not to burn paper excessively, there is little else that can be done without ruffling too many feathers. It is almost as if traditionalists are saying, 'We're happy to have our arts and media censored but please, don't mess with our ancient customs or you'll really upset us.'

Medicine is another area where the aunties and uncles of Singapore still cling to old-fashioned remedies. Some, like acupuncture, have been proven to have positive effects upon the patient and have been implemented in the West but many of these remedies do not work. There is a poster on the wall at my doctor's surgery that urges people not to 'burn the snake' because it is extremely dangerous. It is a belief shared by the older generations that when someone, particularly a small child, has chickenpox, his or her head and tail should be burnt to rid the illness, hence 'burning the snake'. Of course, the ritual does nothing but leave the afflicted with burn marks on his or her stomach and lower back. Despite concerted efforts to improve awareness on the subject, my doctor says he still gets the odd case of someone suffering from both chickenpox and severe burns.

Now, do not get me wrong. There is absolutely nothing inappropriate about taking pride in beliefs and customs as long as they do not cause harm to others. Moreover, it should not be to the exclusion of others. I have had dinner with elderly Singaporeans who revel in telling me how they seldom eat Western food because it is so 'disgusting'. Then five minutes later, they shoot me a look more powerful than a Smith and Wesson just because I happen to mention that I am not too fond of shark's fin soup.

After returning from a holiday to England, an elderly colleague opened a conversation with me by saying, 'What do you *people* eat in England?'

'Why?' I asked, my pride more than just a little bruised.

'Well, there's not much choice is there? It's all chips and sandwiches. How can you live on that stuff all year round?'

I would love to say that I suffocated him with a chip sandwich but I just shrugged my shoulders. What else can you do or say to such a cantankerous old sod?

Despite these shortcomings, the aunties and uncles of Singapore are a warmhearted bunch who will gladly invite you into their home for food during Chinese New Year or Hari Raja celebrations.

If further confirmation of their warmheartedness is needed, I recall an incident that left me stunned. After shopping in Orchard Road with my girlfriend, we got on the MRT train to go to Bishan. The train was relatively packed and I was forced to stand, holding three or four shopping bags. Standing over my better half, we started talking about the usual trivial stuff. As the train pulled into the next station, an elderly Chinese gentleman who had been sitting next to my partner got up and offered me his seat before somebody else nabbed it. I thought this was a most considerate act and I thanked him as he left the train. However, the uncle did not alight.

As the train pulled out of the station, the uncle stood in front of me as large as life, occupying the space where I had previously stood. He had done this either to allow me to sit with my partner or get away from my brain-numbing chatter. In such a situation, you tend to get paranoid. There was a cute little baby sitting on her mother's lap next to me and I swear she would not stop staring at me. I am almost certain that I heard the baby say, 'In my considered opinion, mother, that tall ruffian should have politely refused the elderly gentleman's most generous offer. His ghastly behaviour is so quintessentially English.' To make matters worse, as we passed the next stop, the old man still did not alight. Instead he just stood there, grinning. By this stage, my left ear had begun to melt from all the verbal abuse my girlfriend was inflicting on it. All the stock phrases gushed forth, 'I've never been so embarrassed in all my life…', 'If only you had half a brain' and so on. By now, I wanted to publicly execute my elderly do-gooder just to give me some peace of mind. The man finally alighted at Toa Payoh, having towered over me for a grand total of two stops, during which time I had formulated at least a dozen ways to kill him using one of those flexible hand grips.

In many ways, the elderly are the most appreciative generation of Singaporeans, which, as far as I am concerned, has worrying implications. They still remember the Japanese occupation, the genuine threat of communism and the riots of the 1960s. They are also far more appreciative and respectful of the modern transport services, home ownership and improved medical and educational facilities. The younger generations, just like in England, have no such perspective. They have known only rapid change so it becomes difficult to impress or even pacify them. Tedium inevitably results. When I was at university, I decided to write a thesis on the birth and development of Dagenham, my home town. After interviewing pensioners, I was struck by the deep-rooted pride they still had in the town. They spoke excitedly about how it had taken them from the disease-ridden slums of central London and provided their families with a decent standing of living. For them, that was enough. They were prepared to overlook its shortcomings and the ineptitude of local government. Many have since died, taking their pride to the grave. I believe Singaporean aunties and uncles, by and large, will do the same.

In contrast, the younger generations have no sense of loyalty to their environment. In England, yobs on street corners perceive

Dagenham as both restrictive and boring. Many cannot wait to leave. Having taught at countless schools, I feel that Singaporean youngsters act in the same way. They are not interested in efficient transport services or in Singapore's struggle for economic success. Why should they be? They have known nothing else. I only hope they can learn a sense of perspective from their aunties and uncles before it is too late. There may well be more to life than a train that consistently runs on time but there is categorically more to life than soulless greed. As I sit on the train and watch faceless executives jabber endlessly into handphones, I often wonder how many of them would give up their seat to allow a strange-looking Caucasian to sit next to his partner. I do not kid myself though. I know the answer and so do you. That is the fundamental difference between the generations.

Chapter Three

In Britain, we have curious phenomena that pop up occasionally to make strange sounds and shuffle around bizarrely. They are called grandparents. I often liken them to UFOs because you want to see them, you really do, but you are not sure why. When they are spotted, fear is the first reaction followed by a certain unease that never really leaves until the visit is over. You pretend to understand them but, in reality, you have very few shared interests and you often end up just staring at each other. To top it all off, your grandmother's forehead begins to grow, her face wrinkles quite rapidly and she starts to resemble E.T. In Britain, teenagers and young adults are constantly being reminded to visit their grandparents before they die.

This kind of emotional blackmail seems to be the only way that our dear deceitful mothers can get us to visit our elderly relatives. Well, that is what my mum used. I did love them but watching doddering relatives shuffle around a living room just could not compete with an episode of *Friends*.

My mother and I have acted out the same scenario so many times. She would storm into my bedroom and remind me first of my living arrangements because every conversation we had started this way. She would invariably open with, 'You treat this place like a bloody hotel. You leave your towels on the bathroom floor and you're still not making the bed. I might as well wear a bloody apron.'

At this point, I was always struck by what a boarding house owner would say to his son. 'Now look here, you're treating this place like a bloody hotel and I'm sick of it.'

'But it is a hotel, dad.'

'Don't be so bloody cheeky.' Whack! And so on. And so on for my mum, too.

'Take your feet off the bloody table. You're sitting there like a bloody tramp. And if you have to come in so late, do you have to make so much noise? When are you going to visit your grandparents? They haven't got long left, you know. They're not going to live forever. You're only sitting on your arse, you can go today.'

And that is it, you are sunk. As all teenagers in a similar position will testify, your answering technique, which has been thoroughly honed over the years, brings about your downfall. It usually works to your advantage. Listening for the appropriate pauses in your mother's speech, you deliver the correct expression of consent or disagreement. After a while, the technique has been perfected so it can be performed subconsciously. Complacency inevitably sets in and before you have a chance to retract the answer, the word 'yes' has left your lips and your mother has already pounced. Like a tornado ripping through the house, she has picked out your best clothes, informed her mother that you are coming and dropkicked you out of the house.

Therefore, I hope you see where I'm coming when I say that I had never heard of the term 'filial piety' until I came to Singapore. It means to be a devout or loyal son or daughter or, in broader terms, to respect and look after your family elders. I first came across the term when I was teaching a creative writing course and found it in a narrative written by a primary four pupil. After looking up the meaning of each word, I was stunned that a ten-year-old girl wielded such remarkable vocabulary and I recall giving her a ridiculously high mark. Talking to local colleagues later though, it became apparent that the term was common among Singaporeans, both young and old, because it is a fundamental family value. Filial piety runs right across the racial and cultural spectrum and is encouraged by teachers, religious leaders and politicians alike. In other words, aunties and uncles are protected and looked after, to some degree, by their children and grandchildren, which, in my book, is most praiseworthy.

There is more to it than that, though. Singapore, unlike Britain, is not a welfare state. State pensions and free medical and dental treatment for the elderly do not exist here. Indeed, Lee Kuan Yew, the country's Senior Minister and founder of the People's Action Party, the ruling party of government, does not believe in welfarism. In the book *Lee Kuan Yew: The Man and His Ideas*, he is quoted as saying he believed that the early intentions of welfarism to get Britain back on its feet after the war were honourable. However, he stated that by the 1980s, welfare had undermined the work ethic, creating societies in which people become dependent upon the state rather than upon the fruits of their own labour.

To counter this, Lee has argued many times that individuals work to improve their own lives and those of their families. Therefore, the Singaporean state has made a conscious effort to foster these traditional support systems that are inherent in the Chinese, Malay and Indian communities. Consequently, Singaporeans, in times of trouble, turn to their families and not to the state.

I can already hear my fellow Westerners feverishly picking holes with this argument, dismissing it as ultra right-wing and uncaring. However, without wishing to get bogged down in political arguments, I would like to pick out some of the benefits of such a system. Without fail, my friend David visits his aunties and uncles every Saturday night and he sees nothing irregular in this. For an Englishman like myself, distant aunties are usually only spotted sitting around tables at weddings, gossiping. They do this to keep away from their drunken husbands who are clumsily demonstrating that they can dance like John Travolta – a frequent event at English weddings that is only slightly less embarrassing than watching your aunties trying to dislodge the distant brain cell that contains your name. They usually end up saying, 'Ooh, haven't you grown?' To which you can only retort, 'Well no, I'm twenty-six years old and I haven't grown at all since the last wedding three months ago.'

In contrast, relatives are visited regularly in Singapore and are generally well looked after on birthdays, at festivals and on mahjong gambling days. They are respected members of the family. At the Chinese weddings that I have been to, I have always been introduced to parents, aunties and uncles and grandparents with a discernible sense of pride by my friends. And why shouldn't they be proud of them? In a society that does not support the values of welfarism, they have been clothed, fed and, most importantly, educated by their elders. In recent years, it has become a growing trend to send children overseas for their tertiary education and this does not come cheap. At a conservative estimate, my friend David reckons that his two-year stint at Manchester University would have cost around S$100,000 – not exactly chickenfeed, is it?

This, however, is where filial piety comes into play and it makes me feel just a little nauseous. You see, when parents get to a certain age, it becomes payback time. Their children must begin to look after them financially. Not just because it feels like the right thing to do but because it is a Singaporean custom. In fact, my friend swears that filial piety is a government law. I was sceptical about this. How could such a law be enforced? But I was quite stunned to discover that my friend was right.

In 1995, the Maintenance of Parents Act came into force and a tribunal was set up the following year by the Ministry of Community Development. The act helps parents who are over sixty and unable to support themselves claim maintenance from their children. In other words, elderly parents can sue their children, take them to court and demand that they look after them financially. I had hoped that very few people would need to take advantage of this ingenious piece of legislation but between June 1996 and December 1999, 541 applications were made to the tribunal, of which 404 were ordered to pay maintenance. This may not be a gigantic figure but am I alone in feeling saddened by the news that a court order was needed to remind over 400 citizens that they should be looking after their parents? I cannot help wondering how many more cases there would be if more ill-treated parents took their complaints up with the tribunal. In a society that is obsessed with 'saving face', I am certain that some families keep quiet.

Consequently, it is extremely common, especially when you consider property prices in Singapore, for parents to live with their children's family as they get older, which I believe shows remarkable tolerance on both sides. If my mother and I were to live together again we would, quite simply, kill each other.

I would get up to leave and I would hear her croaky voice ask, 'Where are you going now?'

'I'm going to visit friends. They've just bought a new car.'

'You treat this place like a bloody hotel.'

'Mum, it's my house.'

'You wander in whenever you feel like it. You don't tell me where you've been. I sit here night after night, worrying myself sick, not that you'd care though.'

'Mum, I'm 45 years old. When I go out, it's to collect my children from school.'

'Never mind all that, you're still leaving your towels on the bedroom floor.'

It would be a nightmare and I am sure my mother would agree. But the Singaporeans I know who are married and still live with their parents or parents-in-law bear their hardship with considerable goodwill.

In fact, it appears to be a very amicable relationship. While my friends are out at work, the mother will mop the floors and more often than not prepare meals for them when they return. Of course, I am sure the family picture of idyllic bliss that I have painted is not wholly accurate but I also know that a similar picture in England would have more colourful language.

'Mum,' I would begin tentatively, 'you seem to have more time on your hands since you've moved in with us. Could you help with the housework occasionally?'

'Fuck off.'

End of conversation. Generally speaking, though, this system works for the majority of Singaporeans so where does the nausea that I mentioned earlier come into it? Well, just humour me for a few moments. Can you recall clearly the last time you ate at a greasy burger establishment? Who served you?

Had I asked myself this question before I came to Singapore, the answer would have been a skinny teenage boy wearing a uniform that was made to measure for somebody else. Between serving customers, he would join his other teenage colleagues out back in a 'dipping your head into the deep fryer' contest to determine the greasiest head of hair. Incidentally, I always seemed to be served by the contest winner. Having purchased my food, I would then have to avoid 'greasy head's' twin brother knocking me flat on my face with his lethal combination of a big mop and a tiny brain. Lying on the floor covered in French fries and smelling of detergent, 'greasy head floor cleaner' would always say, 'I'm sorry, I didn't see you there.'

'Why? Because I'm only 6 foot 4 inches tall, you dopey prick,' I would respond. By which time he had already disappeared to take part in the deep fryer semi-finals.

After spending five years in Singapore, the imagery has changed. Instead of the young teenager, you are served by an elderly person, who shuffles slowly to get your order. It was a massive culture shock for me to be served by someone who was older than my grandparents when I first arrived here. I felt so sorry for them as they plodded over to get my order. It made me feel so guilty that I felt as though I should go around the counter and collect the meal myself.

On the plus side, they certainly exude less grease than their Western counterparts and that in itself is a reason to be grateful. But we know the sad reality. When you step into a packed burger bar in Orchard Road and spot three queues of roughly equal size, with two staffed by elderly employees, which line do you pick? In this hectic metropolis obsessed with speed and efficiency, it just would not be practical to be served by some doddering old lady, would it? Particularly when it is obvious that the slimy prick next to her with the artificial smile is just dying to take more orders to demonstrate his robotic speed and his multitasking skills. When I am not in a hurry, I find myself drawn to the elderly employees out of some sort of moral compunction. However, this is Singapore and how often are we not in a hurry?

It seems we are all so busy chasing that all-important dollar that we do not have the time to lift a used tray, walk ten paces to the nearest rubbish bin and empty it. What is the matter with us? I was with a friend once who got up to leave without taking the tray with him. I asked him why and he said, 'That's what they're paid for. Let them do it.' We were sitting three metres away from the nearest rubbish bin and I watched, dumbstruck and ashamed, as a tiny Chinese auntie walked from one end of the restaurant to the other to collect the tray. When she reached our table, she picked up the tray, wiped the table with a cloth and smiled at us. What the hell had we done to deserve such a warm smile? It crushed me. I waited on tables for ten years and hated every single minute of it. I certainly hope I do not have to do it in my sixties, spending my twilight years asking extremely obnoxious customers, 'Upsize for you, sir?' I have never left a tray on a table since.

Therein lies the greatest failing of a society that has no welfare. There is no safety net. I believe in the majority of the PAP's policies but they serve just that – the majority. Most Singaporeans live a safe, clean middle-class lifestyle that is, let's face it, the envy of Southeast Asia and, increasingly, other parts of the world, too. Yet without any form of welfare, there will always be a small number who, through no fault of their own, slip through the net. These people may have little or no family or they might not have the appropriate skills to work in a knowledge-based economy. Pride might also prevent them from dragging their own flesh and blood to the tribunal to demand maintenance.

The government, to its credit, is always coming up with laudable retraining schemes but the people who would benefit most from these schemes are usually preoccupied with the 'little things', like putting food on the table. Do not get me wrong, there is no perfect political system and no one can be completely happy with their lot. I agree with the English philosopher Jeremy Bentham and his famous notion of 'the greatest happiness of the greatest number'. I just do not think that filial piety alone, commendable though it might be, is enough to plug the gaps.

Besides, even if it was, there is still one final problem that I have with it that goes way beyond nausea. Having already mentioned that it becomes payback time for parents when they get old and need to be looked after by their children, the stage is then set for the gut-wrenching sequel 'Payback II – After Death'.

The plot is ever so simple. The main protagonist is the ageing head of the family, who is looked after by all her sons and daughters. During an intense emotional scene, which requires great method acting from the supporting cast, the old woman dies happily, knowing that she had a caring, loyal family. Then the flimsy twist comes. The old woman left behind a pot of money in the form of her apartment, which is now worth a small fortune. It is a flimsy twist because it is always the same. The old woman always dies and she always leaves her apartment behind because no matter how many paper houses she might have burned on this Earth, she cannot physically take her home with her. Then shock horror, all the affectionate relatives suddenly become green-eyed bastards who put up with her for all those years in the belief that she would leave the box of concrete to them.

So the audience, in other words the *Straits Times* readers, is introduced to a plethora of secondary characters who, until this point, had only been spotted buying the old lady the odd meal. Now they come to the fore and cry, 'She promised to leave me the apartment because she loved me the most and she wanted it to stay in the family. However, I really intend to sell the flat when the market peaks for an enormous fat profit. Then I can upgrade to those new condominiums being built on the coast and my shallow, unfulfilled life will finally be complete.' The plot thickens quicker than cold curry when not one but several characters come forward and recite similar well-rehearsed speeches.

At this point, the cynical members of the audience are already questioning the so-called moral values of filial piety. It now seems that the system works like this. You provide your child with the best education because that will improve his and, therefore, your standard of living later on. You then retire and live off your children if they have succeeded in life or, failing that, you take a part-time job mopping toilet floors. Finally, the children that you raised, whether they were successful or not, will all fight for your apartment when you die.

For those who think I am being overtly cynical, just read through the *Straits Times*. On any given day, you are bound to come across a financial or property wrangle between different generations of the same family. They are usually despicable affairs, with both sides washing each other's dirty linen in public in a pathetic bid to be awarded those shares or that luxurious condominium.

In 1998, for example, Janie Low took her father and her brother to the High Court and ordered them to buy over her shares in the family-owned food distribution company. She won the case when the judge discovered that as director, the father had, among other things, abused the company accounts for personal gain by charging holiday expenses to the company. Hence, the judge sided with

Madam Low and ordered her father to buy her shares at a non-discounted rate, which, I am sure, left her an extremely wealthy woman. By this stage, however, there was not much the public did not know about her personal life and her relationship with her father.

Then there was the famous Jumabhoy case, which was so ghastly and dragged on for so long that no one really wants the whole thing regurgitated here. Suffice to say, the Jumabhoys are a prominent Indian family in Singapore. The family's elderly patriarch, Rajabali Jumabhoy, who died two months short of his 101st birthday, sued his eldest son, Ameerali, and two grandsons for allegedly cutting out other family members in running property and hotel group Scotts Holdings. The case went on for years and the family name was dragged through the mud. It was eventually resolved in 1999 when the court ruled against Rajabali's claims. He died shortly after and certain prominent family members are still not talking to each other. Call me naive but I would rather plod along with my middle of the road income than put my family through such a farcical soap opera.

Such high-powered family struggles are by no means exclusive to Singapore. The United States is famous for them. Indeed, if the Jumabhoys had been American, they would have appeared on Oprah Winfrey at least twice and Jerry Springer would have told them to 'put aside their money troubles and bind together through the power of love'.

In Singapore, it is the little cases that sadden me, such as families going to the smaller courts to contest the will of their late father to try to get his old HDB apartment. These incidents occur all the time. When I was renting a room from Saudita, my Indian landlady, she had an Indian friend come and stay with her. She was pathetically frail, at least seventy-five years old and looked as though a strong wind might blow her over. For some strange reason, she was remarkably kind to us. Whenever she went shopping, she would always return with some bananas and insist that we took them. Now I would be lying if I said that I was close to the woman. To this day, I still do not know her name but one Sunday morning, she unfolded a tragic story that will haunt me forever.

Leaving to go over to the local shop, we asked her if she needed anything and she burst into tears. It was obvious that the poor woman desperately needed to confide in someone other than a woman who thought it was acceptable to publicly bare her breasts. So she chose us, which if nothing else, must give an indication of how desperate she was. Like most elderly Singaporeans, she was not well-educated but she and her late husband had worked hard through the years and scraped together enough money to buy a small three-roomed HDB flat. Now a widow, she told us that the flat was hers, lock, stock and barrel. That is when the vultures descended.

Her son and daughter-in-law moved into the flat and kicked her into the smallest bedroom. She did not object. Being a practical woman, she knew she was not going to live forever and the flat would be theirs eventually anyway. Then the problems started. Her daughter-in-law regarded her as no more than an irritant, an obstacle to her owning her own little castle. The arguments started when her daughter-in-law began to dictate the running of the house: when and what its occupants ate, who cleaned the house and so on. Initially, the husband acted as peacemaker. Eventually, he became incensed by his mother's so-called constant nagging. At this stage, the cynical side of me began to think that I had only heard one side of the story. Then she showed us the bruises and I started to get a prickling sensation that ran up and down my spine.

Her puny legs were blackened with dark purple bruises and her upper arms displayed similar marks. She started crying heavily and became almost incoherent. Things had come to a head and her daughter-in-law had beaten her up in her own living room while her husband, the victim's son and heir, watched. The daughter-in-law then threw the old woman out of her own house and onto the street shouting charming things like, 'If you come back here, we'll kill you.' The husband then decided to reveal, for the record, his true feelings on the subject when he got up to assist his wife in the task of kicking his mother out. This happened about a week before she told us the story and the bruises were still there. Since then, the old lady had made just one telephone call to the house, only to be told to 'fuck off' by her son, the person she had raised and clothed.

All of which begs the eternal question: why? Why did she not call the police and have the two greedy fuckers thrown out? Why did she not call the media and have the pair publicly disgraced? Why did she not allow Saudita to remove their limbs? In short, why did she allow them to live rent free in her property while she slept on a mangy old sofa every night, confiding her troubles to two virtual strangers? I asked her all these questions and more, to which she replied, 'He's my son.' What could we say to this? We just cuddled her and left.

That is the major problem I have with filial piety. It relies a little too much on people. Having no welfare means there will always be those who slip through the net and end up serving warm burgers or cleaning toilet floors for ungrateful customers. A chillingly relevant incident occurred outside the Tribunal for the Maintenance of Parents office in 2000. A 56-year-old woman, Chua Bian Neo, was stabbed to death in front of her 89-year-old wheelchair-bound father. She had just attended a hearing at the tribunal with her father to help the old man claim financial aid. The killer was her brother, the very person that she allegedly intended to take to court to get him to help pay a monthly sum for her father's maintenance. It seems that the brother was unhappy with this arrangement so he stabbed his older sister in the back as his disabled father looked on helplessly.

Such incidents are extremely rare in Singapore and I do not want to give the wrong impression of what really is one of the safest countries in the world, but it does highlight one of the fundamental weaknesses of filial piety. Although there is a parliamentary act in place, some people still do not feel obliged to look after their parents. Even the ones that do can sometimes leave you questioning their motives. In a country that is obsessed with property and financial status, there are those who fall victim to greedy, parasitic children. That is why I get just a tad pissed off when I hear the term filial piety. For most people, it conjures up positive images of children supporting their parents in times of need. For me, it reminds me of a frail, weeping old lady showing me the bruises on her legs. And it breaks my heart.

Chapter Four

If there is one thing that I will always express the deepest gratitude for, it is the simple fact that Singaporeans who work in fast-food chains do not sell their own food. If they did, it would take them a lifetime to serve each customer. You see, Singaporeans of all ages, but particularly the elderly, love their grub and like nothing more than to give you the odd morsel of home-cooked food. I can just imagine it.

'Can I have a hamburger, please?' I would begin innocently.

'Certainly, and how about one or two of the curry puffs that I've just made.'

'No, I just want a hamburger, thanks.'

'But you'll love the way that these have been cooked.'

'Okay, I'll take one then, thank you.'

'I'll give you two anyway and some Chinese tea on the side.'

'But I'm not thirsty.'

'Never mind, I made this tea especially. My mother gave me the recipe. It'll stop you catching colds and improve sexual performance.'

'I'll take fifteen cups, please.'

'I'll put in some fried chicken for you, too, to go with the tea.'

'But I'll explode. I couldn't possibly...'

'Well, I've cooked it now. It's my great-grandmother's most famous recipe. Our entire family swears by it. Please take it. Otherwise, I won't be able to sleep tonight.'

You have no choice but to eat all the food, waddle out of the shop, proceed to a discreet corner and die. I know this to be an incontestable fact because I have expired several times after going to a friend's auntie's place to have a wee 'bite to eat'. It is always the same. Taking your place at the table, you are shocked to find that the table has, in fact, disappeared. No one told you that someone in the family was training to be the next David Copperfield. For the table has vanished under a multitude of bowls, plates and cups, all of which are full. Twenty-seven bowls of fifty-three different dishes later, you realise who the magician was. It was the lady of the house who kept whizzing past you to fill the table with various dishes at breakneck speed.

So let's not beat about the bush here. If there is one thing Singaporeans can be truly proud of, it is their dominant food culture that can be traced back to the origins of modern Singapore. When Sir Stamford Raffles was sent by the East India Company in 1819 to find trading outposts along the Straits of Malacca, he saw Singapore and said, 'That one looks fine, I'll take it. Do you take American Express?' Before long, Malays from all over the archipelago, Indians and mainly Chinese all flocked to Singapore to look for work or to trade. By 1841, the population had already passed 40,000 and continued to rise. What did they bring with them in abundance? Their local dishes, of course.

The Malays enriched their spicy dishes with coconut milk sauces. Their *nasi padang*, which is a choice of spicy meat, such as mutton or chicken curry, served with various vegetables on a banana leaf, is my favourite. Beef rendang is also delicious but even that pales in comparison to satay. Whether it be chicken, pork or beef, barbecued satay is one of those things that I could eat all day. Though I would like to point out a little fact to certain food court operators. If hawker centre stall owners can afford to sell satay sticks at 30 cents each, take a little profit and still make them taste divine, why, may I ask, do you have to sell them at 60 cents each? Please do not tell me that your overheads are so high that you must charge almost double for something that costs very little to produce. It is just a little observation that tends to make me say, 'Sixty cents for a stick of fucking satay,' when the mood takes me.

Then there is Indian cuisine. Ever since I was a young boy growing up in Dagenham, I have always had a penchant for Indian food after my mother declared it a Saturday night treat. It became a tradition. In parts of England, we tend to have food traditions.

For example, Friday night is usually fish and chips night. In truth, this was an occasion I dreaded more than I actually enjoyed as my mother would always make me run to the chip shop. She would not allow my younger sister to go to the shopping precinct after dark – an excuse my sister managed to get good mileage out of until she left home at twenty-two, I might add. So it was left to me to perform 'The Sprint' to collect the fish and chips. This involved a beanpole of a teenager, i.e., me, running for his life while holding a bag of piping hot fish and chip meals under his left armpit. Arriving home and breathing like a nymphomaniac, he would muster the strength to knock on the door. His mother would open it and, with a face like thunder, say, 'What took you so long? The chips are freezing cold. Look at them! I'm going to have to microwave them now and you know I hate microwaved chips. I'll go myself next time.'

That was our Friday night food tradition. Our Saturday night treat in later years was one I really did enjoy because it involved Indian food. There would be dishes of chicken briyani, various curries, mutton korma, Bombay potatoes, onion bharjis and piles of naan bread and yellow rice everywhere. After which, the family would sit, motionless and silent, on the sofa watching our stomachs swell and taking turns to either fart or burp. Happy times.

So when I came to Singapore, I was in cuisine heaven. Indians might only make up just over seven per cent of the population but they certainly make their presence felt in food terms. I am told that Northern Indian food is less spicy and uses more cream and ghee whereas Southern Indian dishes favour a greater use of curry leaves, mustard seeds and coconut milk. Ironically, Singapore's most famous Indian dish, fish head curry, is not an Indian dish but rather a regional creation. Still, it typifies local Indian cuisine and I have yet to come across a Singaporean who does not like it. Roti prata, my own favourite Indian dish, is as simple as it is tasty. Looking a little like flat pancakes and slightly bigger than a compact disc, these flour creations are delightful for supper when they are drenched in curry.

The best place to go for any of the above is, without a doubt, Little India in Serangoon Road. When I went to Little India for the first time, I went to Komala Vilas and had the South Indian plate. It was divine. For S$5, you get rice and a series of hot vegetable dishes. The best part is that it is free flowing. You go in, wash your hands, find a table, signal to the old Indian guy to put a banana leaf down and the eating begins. There is no time for any spoon and fork nonsense. I have participated in gluttonous competitions to see who could consume the most food. I must confess that I have never won but I have polished off two full plates of rice, curry and vegetables. Try to top that.

Now, let's talk Chinese. The Chinese are famous worldwide for their cuisines and I would regularly visit my local Chinese takeaway on the way home from the pub. Of course, food always tastes good when you are drunk and if you are really lucky, you get a chance to see it again in the morning. This was why I used to feel so sorry for Chinese restaurant owners in England. They often got to see their well-prepared dishes ten minutes later, usually sprayed up their windows or on the pavement outside their shop. Sometimes, I sit and watch the hawker stall operators and see how hard they work in sweaty conditions. Although they must have a hard life, I still believe that hawker stall workers are better off than those running takeaway restaurants in the inner cities of England.

Chinese restaurant owners in England undoubtedly enjoy a higher standard of living because Chinese food there is not exactly cheap. However, I imagine that around 11 o'clock, when the pubs close, their job becomes hellish. Drunks all over the world are renowned for their lack of charm and sophistication, and some in England would not feel out of place at a Ku Klux Klan meeting. In fact, the *Straits Times* published a report in April 2000 stating that violent attacks on Chinese restaurateurs in London were on the increase and appeared to be racially motivated. To be sure, the Chinese in England make a hell of a lot more money than they would if they ran a hawker stall in Singapore but hawker stall owners do not have to endure racist shit every other night.

This is just as well because it gives these hawker stall owners more time to concentrate on doing what they do best, producing good grub. There are far too many exquisite dishes to be able to list them all here so I will just mention my favourites. You cannot go far wrong if you ask for *char siew fun*, which is barbecued pork rice. I am also a bit of an expert on the old chicken curry, seeing as I eat it at least five times a week (I am not kidding), especially the Chinese version with its hot reddish curry and fat potatoes.

When I eat at a Chinese restaurant, I always get a plate of Chinese mixed vegetables regardless of what else I order. This dish includes carrots, broccoli, mushrooms, cauliflower and heaven knows what else and is cooked and served in an oyster sauce. I could eat it all day, along with ginger beef, which is strips of tender beef served with ginger and spring onion and cooked in a thick oyster sauce.

I suppose the best thing about Chinese food, and this is going to sound awfully obvious, is that it is so varied. With so many Chinese immigrants arriving in the 1820s to escape the poverty, famine and political unrest in China, Singapore soon became home to Hokkiens, Cantonese, Teochews and the many other Chinese provincials who joined the country's Straits Chinese. Yet if I had to highlight just one group of Chinese settlers for their dish, it would have to be the Hainanese for their chicken rice. For my money, if one dish were to symbolise and represent Singaporean cuisine, it would have to be this one. Its tender chicken is either boiled or roasted, cut into strips and placed across the best-tasting rice in, well, the universe. Cooked in chicken stock that is also served as soup, it is the fluffiest, juiciest rice in the business.

However, do not think that it is just the French who stuff their faces with frog's legs. There are several hawker centres and coffee shops that I have been to that keep dozens of live frogs in a tank for you to select from. I speak from experience here. After being in Singapore for about three days, David took Scott and me out for a late night supper and placed a mysterious dish in front of us that looked like undernourished chicken wings fried in batter. The titbits did not taste too badly. They tasted like greasy chicken but with very little meat around the bone. Of course, David then pointed out the tank containing the frogs and laughed – Singapore 1 England 0. Consequently, Scott and I made up some stories about the ingredients that went into some of the famous English dishes that we knew David had tried at Manchester. Let's just say that when he visits England again, I do not think that he will be eating shepherd's pie, toad in the hole or spotted Dick in a hurry.

There are two things to learn from this. First, the English do, to their credit, have some wonderfully eccentric names for their dishes. I believe this is to compensate for the fact that we do not have very many so we tend to go a bit overboard on our culinary creations.

Second and perhaps far more relevant, the extent and choice of dishes cannot be overstated in Singapore. I have barely scratched the surface with the few that I have mentioned. Despite its small size (it is only 641 square kilometres), Singapore has Thai stalls, Indonesian restaurants, Japanese sushi bars and places where you can get Vietnamese, Korean or even Mongolian food. Then around places like Holland Village, the so-called sophisticated area where all the expatriates hang out, there are Mexican, Mediterranean, Middle Eastern and even German restaurants. A food haven for the fussiest of Western tourists.

I feel, however, that I should point out a little observation about Western food served at hawker stalls. You see, it is not really Western food at all or it certainly is not English food. Whenever I walk past the food stalls in a coffee shop and I pass a Western stall, the owner will invariably say, 'Hello, sir. Chicken chop for you, sir?' This always makes me laugh. You see, call me uncultured but I had never even seen a chicken chop before I came to Singapore, let alone eaten one. I confess I am no English aristocrat but even this working-class urchin has eaten at cafés, restaurants and the odd hotel and yet I had never come across a chicken chop and nor had any of my friends. Pork chops, yes, and, of course, we had all eaten lamb chops but never a chicken one. Despite this fact, nearly every single Western stall in Singapore sells them. There is a stall in Toa Payoh Lorong 1 where the friendly owner actually calls me 'chicken chop'. At first, I thought he was asking me if I wanted a chicken chop but I realised he was, in fact, calling me one.

I would approach the stall and he would shout, 'Wah, chicken chop, what you want today?'

'Egg and bacon, can?'

'Can lah, chicken chop, no problem.'

Sure enough, eggs and bacon would arrive and that would be it. In fact, the eggs and bacon would arrive with cucumber and lettuce, a strange but refined addition to the traditional English breakfast. It is all delicious but I just cannot help wondering where the stall owners get their recipes from.

Eating out in Singapore is a social occasion whereas it is something that is done out of necessity in England. That is not to say that English people do not enjoy fine dining, we love our grub as much as the next overweight Western consumer. As a rule, however, the restaurant is not our major forum for social interaction, the pub is. Hence, Singapore has a food culture; England has a pub culture.

When I was eighteen, my step-dad was giving me a lift home one night when we passed the Robin Hood pub in Dagenham, which was notorious for its unruly clientele. As we pulled up at the traffic lights, we saw two guys fighting each other with snooker cues outside probably the world's shittiest pub. What I remember vividly about the incident was that it was only 10 o'clock in the evening and these two guys were openly brawling. Even more striking was the reaction of my stepfather, which was nothing. Having grown up in West London, he had seen it so many times before that he just made some passing comment about 'those silly bastards' and looked away. I was stunned. It was like a scene from Martin Scorsese's *Mean Streets*. The two guys were ripping lumps out of each other's backs while men and women just stood and watched. It really was nothing out of the ordinary.

That is certainly one advantage of having such a thriving food culture. You seldom hear of Singaporeans having a brawl outside a food court because they have both eaten too much nasi padang. The only violence I have encountered at a restaurant is me hitting companions with noodles as I fight a losing battle with a pair of chopsticks. I am hopeless with chopsticks. I have all the control of a baby holding a marker pen. I can just about manage the wooden ones but when it comes to those heavy silver ones you get in hotels, well, you might as well give me a pair of javelins.

Having such a dominant food culture does have its drawbacks though. An expatriate friend was on his way home from work one day when he decided to pop in on his Chinese girlfriend for a chat. Being polite, he called her first to let her know he was coming and told her that he had already eaten.

When he arrived, he discovered to his horror that her parents had kindly prepared him a meal. As you can imagine, there was plenty there. He sat down at the table and looked down at the food. He tried to muster the energy to eat it but he could not. His girlfriend urged him to make an effort because her parents had taken the time to cook it and he would offend them. A valid point. My friend then explained that he had just wolfed down a substantial meal and although he was extremely grateful to her parents and did not want to upset them, he had not asked them to prepare a meal in the first place. An equally fair point.

The girlfriend's mother then noticed that my friend was not eating his meal and had a discreet word with her daughter. The girlfriend then told my friend that her mother was a little upset because he was not making an effort. By this stage, the atmosphere was souring rapidly and what had seemed to be a rather trivial matter to him was on the verge of becoming serious. The parents told their daughter that although they understood that her boyfriend had already eaten, he was insulting them by not even trying the food and that he must at least attempt to eat it. When my friend heard this, he actually laughed at the incredulity of it all, which only served to piss off his peacekeeping girlfriend. Exasperated, my friend shovelled down forkfuls of what he later described as the most uncomfortable meal of his life. He spent most of a miserable evening at the girl's house avoiding her parents and then spent an even more miserable night on the toilet. Apparently, relations between all four protagonists cooled so drastically that it was several weeks before the matter was eventually resolved when my friend apologised.

Make of this incident what you will. Some would say it was a culture clash; that my friend was intolerant or the girl's parents too stubborn. Others would argue that the whole episode is stunningly trivial and overblown. I would side with this viewpoint if it had been an isolated incident. But it is not.

During our first week in Singapore, Scott and I were taken to an auntie's house for a meal and as always the dishes were delightful. All except one – peanut soup. Along with David's homemade shark's fin soup in Manchester, peanut soup is the worst thing that I have ever tasted. Perhaps it was our Western palates stubbornly refusing to acclimatise to a unique taste but the soup affected Scott particularly badly. No one else noticed but I saw him shudder as he swallowed it.

Now there should be nothing wrong with this. I have yet to meet a person who has liked absolutely everything that he has tasted. After all, we are only human. And I would wager that no one would actually enjoy my mother's baked potatoes with their razor-sharp, slit-your-throat edges. But as we sat at the dinner table, Scott and I were made to feel most uncomfortable. Our hostess insisted several times that we drank the soup so we grew to like it. Scott bore the brunt of it. He was hemmed in by over-eager aunties who watched him eat every mouthful. Luckily, I was sitting at the other end of the table where I had perfected the unoriginal technique of holding a glass of water in one hand and a spoonful of peanut soup in the other. When no one was looking, I would swallow the soup and then hose down my taste buds before they could cry 'What the fuck are you doing to us?' Scott had no chance. He drank at least half the soup before he was left alone. Back at home later that night, he spent over an hour redecorating the inside of our toilet bowl with the soup. Two years later, after he had returned to England, I met up with him and brought up the subject of peanut soup. With no hesitation, he said, 'I can still remember the taste of that stuff. I thought it was gonna fucking kill me.' Quite.

This is the fundamental problem with having such a proud, dominant culture of any kind: there will always be a fine line between pride and arrogance. Walk into any pub in England and tell the landlord that his beer is the worst you have ever tasted and you will not leave with a friendly pat on the back.

When my dad was drunk, he would champion the quality of British beer. 'Son,' he would say, 'I've said it before and I'll say it again. He might have played for Manchester United but George Best was the greatest.'

'Yes, dad. He could do it all, couldn't he, dad?'

'He could do it all, boy. He could shoot, head, dribble, cross, pass and he could get stuck in and tackle with the best of them.'

'Better than Pelé, dad?'

'Better than Pelé, boy. He could do it in all weathers: rain, sleet, snow, sun and gale force winds.'

'Strange weather in Manchester, dad?'

'That's right. And I'll tell you another thing. Never, ever, wear white towelling socks with trousers. That is bad dress sense. Never do it.'

'You're right, dad.' I would be fighting sleep by this stage. But when he paused to smile lovingly at his pint glass, I knew my night was over.

'But best of all, there's nothing in the world like a pint of beer. You could travel the world and never get a decent, cold pint like you can in Britain. British beer is something to be proud of. No one can make beer like we can.' He would then go and order a pint of Heineken beer, which is about as British as tulips and windmills.

Singaporeans, by and large, are the same with food. Food is considered to be superior so it must be eaten. This is in stark contrast to the British, largely because the British know, subconsciously, that they cannot cook. To get around this failing, they will beg you not to eat their food. My mother was brilliant at this. I would bring a friend to dinner and my mum would cook a meat pie and plenty of gravy to soothe our hard palates, which would be cut to ribbons by her potatoes with the razor-sharp edges. She would place the food on the table, which I knew had taken her an hour to prepare, and order my guest not to eat it.

She would say, 'There you go, Ross. Now if there's anything you don't like, just leave it on the side of your plate. Don't be shy.'

'Okay, thanks, Sue,' my friend Ross would reply, raising his cutlery eagerly, blissfully ignorant of the bloody massacre that awaited the roof of his mouth. Then my dear mother would start again.

'I mean it, Ross. If there's anything you don't want, just leave it on your plate. Don't think that I'll say anything, I won't mind. Please Ross, don't eat my dinner, I know you won't like it. Come on, I'll throw it away and we'll order a pizza.'

Of course, I would go over to Ross's house for dinner and his mother would similarly beg me to do the same. Mothers up and down the British Isles are right now ordering their guests not to eat their food. Meanwhile, your fathers and uncles are dragging you over to the local pub and forcing you to drink beer for the first time, even though it tastes like liquefied ashtrays. It is most ironic.

That is the price you pay for growing up in a country that has a thriving pub culture. Just as having an auntie zealously cajoling you into drinking peanut soup is the price you pay for living in a society where its people pride themselves on their cuisines. I know that there are Singaporeans who will only consider the Asian dishes on a restaurant menu, no matter where they are. And these are, inevitably, the same morons who will raise an eyebrow should I have the audacity to turn down a bowl of peanut soup.

Thankfully, though, this dogmatic attitude is evolving and giving way to a more cosmopolitan outlook. Younger Singaporeans now go to pubs to sample traditional Western fare such as bangers and mash or shepherd's pie. They are just as comfortable with a plate of spaghetti bolognaise as they are with a bowl of tom yam soup. This is the only way to go.

To be fair, not every Singaporean force-feeds you something you do not like and not every British drinker ends up fighting with a snooker cue. At this point in time, however, I know which culture I prefer. Where else in the world can you find such variety, such choice and at such low cost? Singaporeans should take pride in their food because, unlike Heineken 'British' beer, it really does belong to them. I am forever hearing about Singaporeans trying to build their own identity. Well, if their national cuisine is not a valid starting point, then frankly, I do not know what is. It does not matter where the dishes originated from, the likes of chicken rice, satay and fish head curry are now as Singaporean as the Merlion. And the best thing about local food is that whenever I sit down to eat in a hawker centre, I do not have to suffer my dad's drunken ramblings about George Best, white socks and the merits of British-Dutch beer. Now that is a cause for genuine gratitude, wouldn't you agree?

Chapter Five

I will never understand what it is that draws me to chicken restaurants. The chicken, though undoubtedly tasty, is greasy and runs down the back of your hand and along your forearm, which is the most uncomfortable feeling in the world when you are wearing a long-sleeved shirt on a humid day. Instinctively, you reach for a napkin but, naturally, you have only been given two and they were both used on the first piece of chicken. You then have no choice but to turn to the mashed potato, which resembles baby food and is about as filling. Yet despite these irritants, we still find ourselves drawn to the smell of fried chicken. So there I stood one afternoon at the counter of such a restaurant in Toa Payoh, waiting to place my order. I remember vividly being served by an extremely attractive Malay teenager. 'She will break a few hearts one day,' I thought to myself. Five minutes later, I would have happily broken her neck.

'Can I have a two-piece baby food set, please?' I asked politely.

'One original set. Anything else?'

'No. But can I change my drink to Sprite, please?'

She started giggling at this apparently hilarious request. 'I'm sorry. What drink you want again?'

'Sprite, please.'

More giggles. 'Wah, your English so funny. You not English, is it?'

'Yes, I am. I am also an English teacher so could you tell me what is so wrong with the way I speak?'

Now this may seem a trifle aggressive but it is most irritating having someone laugh in your face. Besides, my accent has always been a cause for a little paranoia. Being a working-class lad, my cockney accent was certainly not the most common accent heard along the corridors of Manchester University so a little insecurity is inevitable. Having undergone phonetics training for my job, I knew that my pronunciation of the word 'sprite' was correct. I mean, as English words go, it is hardly supercalifragilisticexpialidocious, is it? But the counter girl had not finished.

'The way you say "splat" so funny, loh.'

'What? The way I say it correctly, you mean?'

'But you don't. You say "sprite" and I say "splat". It's really funny.'

'My chicken's getting cold and my baby food's melting. Do you think I could get my "splat" now?'

'Yes, of course.' With that, she went over to the drinks machine and filled my cup up with 'splat'. I thanked her for pointing out the gross imperfections of my English and soaked her with the 'splat'. That was as far as it went. To this day, it remains the most serious direct run-in I have had with a Singaporean youth. Just a little bit of playful cheek. No aggression, no bad language, no knives being held to my friend's throat, in fact, nothing more than innocent sauciness.

This contrasts sharply with the youngsters I grew up with in Dagenham. When I was fifteen, my good friend Ross was walking home from school when two young boys walked towards him and got his attention with the audacious shout of 'Oi!' Giggling, the small one piped up. 'Will you tell your mum to stop changing her lipstick?'

'Why?' Ross asked innocently.

'Because it's making my cock multicoloured.' They both laughed hysterically and walked on.

Ross merely laughed to himself and he told me all about the episode the next day at school. I laughed as well. Then he told me that both boys could not have been more than six years old so I laughed again. It made the story even funnier.

These were the kind of youngsters I grew up with. Sitting in a science class in secondary two, I was tapped on the shoulder by David, one of the class bullies. Turning slowly, I was greeted by the sight of an erect penis. David was having a sizing contest with Gary, another school bully, and they wanted an independent arbitrator to ... well, arbitrate. David gestured towards his exposed anatomy. He held a ruler in the other hand.

'Well, what do you think?' he asked excitedly.

'About what?'

'Look, Gary reckons his is bigger than mine. But have a look, mine is over six inches. His is nowhere near that size. He's got a tiny knob. Mine's definitely bigger, isn't it?'

'I don't know, do I? I haven't seen his, have I?'

'Oh yeah. Well, come to the back of the class, he's got his out. You can measure it. No problem.'

'No! I'm not measuring anybody's knob, all right?'

'But mine's definitely bigger than six inches, right?'

'If you say so. But don't expect me to put a ruler against it.'

'I knew it was bigger than six inches. Cheers, Neil. Oi Gary! I told you mine was bigger than yours. Your knob's tiny.'

I could fill a whole book with childhood stories like that. I have told a few to some Singaporean friends and it is interesting to watch their stunned expressions. Instinctively, they assume I am lying. They want me to tell them I am lying to reassure them. Partly because the London they know is the one that has the Queen, fish and chips, famous castles and quaint little bookshops in places like Notting Hill that are owned and run by gentlemen like Hugh Grant. They want to believe this so that they can cling to the ridiculous notion that Britain is a green and pleasant land, a positive place of democracy and free speech. In short, a society fit for the disillusioned Singaporean. Surely, they assume, such incidents do not occur in Britain? They are not allowed to. Surely, the teacher, the parent, the policeman or the politician would step in to check this anti-social behaviour as they do in Singapore?

The fact remains, though, that these incidents do occur among the youth in the West from time to time. Whereas I am fairly certain, having taught in Singapore for over two years, that they do not here. Call me old-fashioned but I have never seen a penis in a Singaporean classroom. Although I have been called a penis.

Teaching speech and drama to a nursery class a couple of years ago, I would line the children up at the end of every lesson and say goodbye. As each child went out, he or she would say, 'Bye Mr Bean' and giggle. I was a bit of a clown and it was a harmless nickname. One day, Malvin, a cheeky little chap, sprang a new term on me that left the rest of the class in stitches. He shouted, 'Bye-bye Mr Cuckoo Bird.'

Initially, I thought 'cuckoo bird' was a bizarre name to bestow upon a teacher but I did not give it much thought. However, when it reached the point where the whole class would cry 'Bye Mr Cuckoo Bird' in chorus and then leave the room with tears rolling down their cheeks, I knew something was seriously amiss. I found myself in one of those uncomfortable situations that are abhorred universally. I did not know something. How could I approach a colleague, a fellow teacher I might add, and ask him what a seemingly common noun meant? In my experience, teachers will remove their genitalia with a blunt instrument before admitting that they do not know something.

In the end, though, it bordered on the ridiculous. As the pupils left the class one by one, I started to notice that the parents were also giggling. I had no choice but to seek the truth and my attempts to do so can only be described as pathetic. Sidling up to the administrative staff after lessons one evening, I adopted my puzzled look.

'You know,' I started, 'you get a lot of birds in Singapore, don't you?'

'Yes, you do,' replied Chris, one of the admin girls, in a tone that suggested she had never heard such a dull question in her entire life.

'But you don't get cuckoos, right?'

'I don't think so.'

'Erm, cuckoo bird, cuckoo bird. It's strange.' I muttered aloud.

'Why are you saying those words?' Chris asked, giggling.

'Oh, for no reason. I saw this Singaporean documentary about wildlife last night and they kept referring to this "cuckoo bird" and it was a bit confusing.'

'Did they? Which programme was it?'

'Oh, it was that one on wildlife. I can't remember what time it was on.'

'Really? I didn't see it in the paper. What channel was it on?' She knew I was lying through my teeth.

'Okay, my children keep calling me Mr Cuckoo Bird and it makes them laugh hysterically. I have no idea what it means but it's got to the stage where I've caught their parents sniggering too. Quite frankly, it's beginning to irritate me. So if you know what it means, please put me out of my misery. If you don't, stop giggling.'

'It's a penis,' said Chris, like it was the most obvious answer in the world.

'It's a what?'

'It's a man's penis. You know?'

'Yes, I know what a man's penis is. Are you telling me that my nursery children have been calling me Mr Penis every week?'

'Well, yes. Cuckoo bird sounds like the word for "penis" in one of the dialects.' Inevitably, Chris found this a reason for much merriment and I became the penis man in the office for quite some time thanks to those adoring little bastards.

Penises aside, Singaporean youngsters were a pleasure to teach. I had only been in Singapore for a month when I was thrown in at the deep end and sent to teach at Victoria School. Victoria, or VS as it is more popularly known, is considered one of the best boy schools in Singapore. On my first day, I was standing outside my classroom and generally being nosy when a student passed.

'Good morning sir,' he said breezily.

'Hello,' I replied. 'Do you know me?'

'No, sir.'

'Am I teaching you this term?'

'I don't think so, sir.'

'Then why did you greet me just now?'

'Oh, we greet every teacher we meet, sir. See you.'

'Yes, see you.' I was stunned. With the exception of some of the better state and private schools in England, this kind of behaviour is not common. Such incidents were not exclusive to VS, though. Each school I have taught at, be it primary or secondary, neighbourhood or independent, I have always encountered extremely polite, conscientious pupils. There were, of course, one or two rare exceptions but they were never difficult to teach.

Without doubt, I sympathise with schoolchildren here because they are under such tremendous pressure to deliver the academic goods. From the day they can talk until the day they graduate from university, their parents are always just one step behind, prodding them forward. I think it is fair to say that when it comes to a child's education, the parents want the best that their money can buy. Not an unreasonable supposition, perhaps. However, there is a twist. The investor wants to see an academic return or someone, somewhere down the line, is going to get it.

When I was teaching, I often took calls from parents who were interested in enrolling their children for speech courses. A parent once asked if she could put her child, who had just won a public speaking competition at school, into one of our oral communication examination classes. These classes involved reciting poetry, drama passages and speeches from memory. I suggested that the child was too young. The classes were mixed in terms of age and ability so it was highly possible that the girl could be in a group with teenagers aged fifteen or sixteen. The mother was adamant that her child would manage because she was 'a very bright girl'.

After speaking to my boss, I came back to the phone and told the mother that her child really would not be able to cope with such group dynamics. She then scolded me over the phone, telling me that I had no right to pass judgement on her child without assessing her capabilities. I said that I did not have to. The girl was four years old. She was nearing the end of kindergarten one (K1) and her mother was demanding that she be put in a class with teenagers and entered for oral examinations. Words cannot aptly describe such imbecilic behaviour. The sad fact is that we had parents like that walk into our office almost every week. The neurotic mother eventually relented and the girl ended up in one of my classes. She was intelligent and her vocabulary was way ahead of her peers. She lived for the worksheets and the homework but when it came to interactive conversations about *Tellytubbies, Sesame Street* and *Star Wars*, she would withdraw and become distant.

That is the tragic compromise that many Singaporean children are subconsciously forced to make. When you are being shunted from one private lesson to another and from one textbook to another, how much socialising do you actually have time for? The sad fact is that textbook examination-oriented learning from such an early age rarely makes for riveting conversation and it is becoming increasingly difficult to see where these children's social skills are going to come from.

I have lost count of the number of times that I have stepped into a secondary school classroom in Singapore and been greeted by twenty academic shells. They are highly efficient robots who have been trained to reproduce information while travelling along the production line of examinations. It was soul destroying. I watched their expressionless faces and I could see that they could not compute the value of speech and drama. After all, it had no examination at the end of the course, no certificate and no promises of a highly paid job so the subject seemed illogical to them.

Gradually, the students would open up and they began to see the class as a welcome bonus in their timetable rather than a hindrance that stopped them from getting their maths homework done. I am not going to lie and say that I was Robin Williams and by the end of the course, the class resembled a scene from *Dead Poet's Society*, with them all vowing to be actors, singers and writers. The majority will still end up in the marketing or electronics sector because they have too many other influences to contend with. Despite watching academic shells blossom into more confident individuals in my class, I was resigned to the fact that they still had to produce results once they left. But at what cost?

In one drama lesson at VS, I caught a secondary two boy sleeping. He was not just dozing, he was in one of those 'I'm in such a deep sleep that I would barely notice if you ripped my vital organs out' types of sleep. In fact, it was his snoring that brought him to my attention. Without wishing to embarrass the boy further, I asked to see him at the end of the lesson.

After class, he apologised sincerely and promised that it would never happen again. After considerable prompting, the boy told me that he had been up until 2:30 a.m. that morning doing his homework. As he got up at 6 a.m. to come to school, the boy had only had three hours sleep. Moreover, he had been staying up late for most of that week to get all his homework completed. The poor boy was under intense pressure at home to lift his marks as one or two of his recent test performances had been deemed below par by his parents. He was thirteen. Bearing in mind it was around February and the school year was just two months old, I asked him what kind of academic work was so important that a thirteen-year-old boy had gone without sleep? After all, he was not doing his degree finals or writing a PhD thesis, he was just doing run-of-the-mill school homework. Yet the lad felt obligated to push himself to the limit to satisfy those around him, even if it meant snatching sleep during one of my lectures on Stanislavsky's method acting. The poor sod did not know what he was missing.

The worst part is, of course, we all know that he is not an exceptional case. I recently read a story in the *Straits Times* about the latest batch of O level results. Make no mistake, the majority of Singaporean students performed extremely well and ended up with a long list of As and A+s, which is undoubtedly impressive. However, my attention was drawn to the photographs, which accurately depicted the joy and despair of successful and slightly less successful (after all, there is no need to use the 'f' word here) students. In both pictures, the teenagers were crying. In the case of those who did not perform so well, the reasons were obvious. But tears were still shed by those who had achieved straight As. It was only after I had read one or two of the quotes that the penny dropped. The word 'relief' kept cropping up. On several occasions, students who passed with flying colours spoke of relief before they spoke of joy. The pressures must have been unbearable.

Of course, this is the case for students in any country. I remember the relief I felt when my GCSE results were satisfactory. However, there was one crucial difference. That relief was a result of pressure I had applied on myself. My parents trusted that I would perform to the best of my ability and left it to me. Not a single tear was shed over an exam result and my school had the dubious honour of churning out some of the worst GCSE and A level results in England.

That is how life was in Dagenham. Education did not and still does not have the prestige that it has in Singapore. Parents simply do not put such store in it. Their rationale is that there will always be enough jobs to go around as there was in their day. Such an easy-going, working-class upbringing does have one major advantage: social skills come in abundance.

If Singaporeans of all ages have one failing, it is that they are not streetwise enough. This rare type of intelligence is developed in most English children when they are very young. The sharp, fast-talking language of the living room is soon transferred to the school playground, the local park and then the street. English kids spend far too much time together messing around when they should be at home studying. That goes without saying. However, constantly being around their peers both in and out of school improves their communicative skills tremendously. Walk around any housing estate in Singapore at 8 p.m. and how many groups of kids do you see hanging out? Not too many because they are at home learning about the basics of supply and demand for an economics project.

I do not doubt for a second that if you pitted an average Dagenham classroom against an average Singaporean classroom in a general knowledge test, the results would be painful. The Singaporeans would win hands down. However, if the two groups were put together after the test and given the chance to chitchat, I am certain that the conversation would be extremely one-sided. I have lost count of the times that I have played 'Just a Minute' in class, a game where you speak spontaneously on a given subject for one minute, and been left wanting to scream. Singaporean youngsters are just not used to speaking freely. If given fun subjects like 'hairy armpits', 'bananas' or 'why I love *Baywatch*', they just freeze. If, however, I give them subjects like 'the Internet', 'computers' or 'Singapore', they simply regurgitate the relevant encyclopaedic entry for sixty seconds. In contrast, a typically brash Dagenham teenager will happily waffle away about bananas for hours. Yet I know that the former will end up earning US$10,000 a month working in property while the latter will probably end up in an office performing clerical duties.

This lack of social skills is about as worrying as it gets as far as Singaporean teenagers go, so allow me the odd chuckle when I hear friends talk about teenage gangsters here. My friend David is always reminding me to stay away from these dangerous gangsters who stalk the streets. These people are apparently so menacing that they have even been labelled with menacing names. The boys are called Ah Bengs and the girls Ah Lians. I have been warned by friends never to make eye contact with them, never to laugh at their ridiculous clothing combinations (white, skin-tight trousers and vest, black belt and a bright yellow handphone stuck to the hip) and never to get into an argument with them because they are usually armed with knives or, wait for it, parangs. Now this last statement floored me. A parang is like a huge sword and something similar to what we call a scythe in England. It is a truly lethal weapon. Think then about these Ah Bengs and their choice of clothing. Believe me, if it is not tight, they will not wear it, so could somebody please tell me where in the name of Al Capone are they going to hide a parang? Do they put it down their trousers and just pretend that they are pleased to see you?

At this point, Singaporeans may feel entitled to stand up and cry that I am addressing an extremely serious social issue in a flippant manner. There are a number of teenage crimes, often committed by these so-called Ah Bengs and Ah Lians. In January 2000, a lawyer was beaten up by a gang of teenagers outside a cinema in front of his wife. It was not a random attack. During the movie that he had just watched, the lawyer had asked one of the gang to stop talking on his handphone as it was disturbing and irritating the rest of the audience. The whole of Singapore, including me, applauded the lawyer for his actions. This anti-social handphone behaviour is driving the country crazy.

After the lawyer asked the teenager to stop informing the entire cinema how he had just spent Christmas, the gangly youth brooded in silence. Then, after carefully checking he had at least three to one odds, the anti-social phone guy cornered the lawyer outside. The lawyer's wife was held back while the rest of the gang gave him a good hiding before running off. The general public was outraged but, thanks to the extremely efficient law and order infrastructure here, the gang was soon rounded up and charged.

Such incidents occur occasionally and they jar the nation and remind its people that they are not invulnerable to crime, despite living in one of the safest countries in the world. These crimes also remind politicians, teachers and parents to reinforce positive social values into their children and to reiterate the dangers of going off the rails and the punishments that will result from a life dedicated to crime. Generally though, everyone tends to get a wee bit carried away as the majority of Singaporean youngsters are a decent lot.

To be reminded of the startling contrast, I need only read a copy of the *Dagenham Post*. My mother sends me a copy of my home town's local newspaper once a month so I can keep tabs on what is happening at home. You would assume that I could just click onto the paper's web site and read about the latest events in Dagenham from here but, alas, the *Post* is not yet online. No surprise there, I know of Dagenham residents who are still struggling with calculators.

The paper's content usually provides an unwelcome jolt back to reality and reminds me of what I have left behind. The lead story on page two of a recent copy was about a teenage mother who was once a heroin addict but had just succeeded in kicking the habit to look after her young son. She then died from an epileptic fit, hence the story. Now be honest, how many similar stories have appeared in either the *Straits Times* or the *New Paper*? The most alarming fact to remember is that this is just a small local paper that covers just one of the thirty-three Greater London boroughs.

In that same edition, the *Dagenham Post* reported a court story that involved grievous bodily harm. The incident was pretty gruesome. A couple in their mid-twenties had an argument in The Pipers, one of the most notorious pubs in Dagenham. The row was disturbing another group of people so one person from the group told the couple to shut up. Dean, the man who was arguing with his girlfriend, took offence to this interference and pushed a glass into the face of the man who had told them to be quiet. He, in turn, took offence to this, mysteriously produced a penknife and stabbed Dean. In fact, he stabbed him so many times that Dean could actually see his own intestines.

There were two things that immediately struck me upon finishing this story. First, the story was tucked away somewhere after page ten, indicating that the editor had realised that its news value, in a Dagenham context, was nothing extraordinary.

The second thing was that I actually knew Dean, the 'ooh, I think I can see one of my intestines' guy. I went to the same school as him. I only knew him because we both needed to take the train to get to school and his younger brother, Dennis, was in my year. Being reasonably close to his brother meant that I was usually spared from the bullying that would be routinely dished out to the other boys who took the train to and from school. His favourite pastime was to lift new students and plonk them onto the railway tracks as the train approached in the distance.

In stark contrast, his younger brother was quiet, placid and could not say words that began with 'sn' properly. For three years,

I would use his speech impediment to break the monotony of the train journey home. After which the poor sod moved with his dad and scumbag brother to an even rougher council estate because they could not maintain the rent payments. When the two boys were younger, their mother had died of a brain haemorrhage in front of them. Admittedly, it must have been an awful childhood but at least the younger brother proved that it did not have to end up with a knife in the guts. You do not come across many youngsters like these two in Singapore, yet when I grew up in England, I went to school with quite a few.

So I remain convinced that the way things stand currently, Singapore has little to fear from its younger generations. They respect family ties and values, are dedicated students (perhaps too dedicated) and cause few disciplinary problems. However, I cannot say that Singapore has nothing to fear.

Young Singaporeans are spoilt. No, let me rephrase that. The majority of Singaporean children rank among the most pampered children on the planet. Unlike their parents and grandparents, most young Singaporeans have experienced nothing but economic growth. Their childhood has been one of continual housing upgrading, decent education, modern shopping centres and fat *hong baos*, or red packets containing money that are given out at Chinese New Year. It does not take a sociologist to realise that such a comfortable lifestyle will have detrimental side effects.

In my classroom, I once had to pull a five-year-old boy away from his maid. He was kicking her because she had forgotten to bring his toys. On another occasion, my colleague Lawrence told me about a ten-year-old girl who submitted a composition about the family's maid. In the piece, she detailed the poor woman's incompetence and how she was so stupid because she did not always obey the instructions given by the girl. Lawrence consulted the girl's mother about the 'Why I hate maids' composition. She just sighed and said, 'But the maid is so damned lazy.'

If this is the attitude that is being instilled into Singaporean children, then the future is bleak. If they grow up believing that they must treat their family with respect but everybody else can be treated shabbily, then we have got a problem. If they also believe that the pursuit of money is the only pursuit in life, then I shudder at the consequences. I have come across enough brain-numbingly boring executives, with a fat wallet and a fast car, to last me a lifetime. These people are never satisfied. They buy a four-roomed flat, then they want a five-roomed one. They buy their first car, which has to be replaced by a Mercedes within five years. Their boss plays golf (squash is now so passé) so they buy a set of clubs and take lessons. It is unoriginal, predictable and depressing. As all of these pursuits take up so much time, they get the maid to wash the car because that is what she is paid for while they get an auntie to clear away their tray in a fast-food restaurant. Then, when they have children, they send them for extra tuition to keep them occupied. The children get everything they want because it appeases them and they shout at the maid because they have seen their parents do it. Suddenly, we have come full circle – Singaporean greed has reproduced itself in the next generation.

As today's teenagers become adults, they are understandably restless and ambitious. The prospect of having a modest flat, a maid and a small car does not pacify them because it is nothing new. So they either go out to chase the dollar at any cost or they emigrate.

I watched Prime Minister Goh Chok Tong give a speech to students a while back urging those who decided to study overseas to enjoy themselves but to make sure they came back to ply their skills here. He sounded like he was almost pleading with them and I cannot say I blame him. When I was teaching, students used to tell me how lucky I was to have grown up in England and how much more exciting it must have been. I used to tell them one or two not-so-good stories from my childhood, adding that the chances of similar incidents occurring here were almost negligible. In a nutshell, schoolchildren are better off here.

Of course, Singaporeans may not be the most socially adept youngsters in the world and children here are expected to work far too hard. Paradoxically, English pupils do not hit the books half as much as they should, yet they are never short of an answer or two in the street. It is a classic case of swings and roundabouts. If I had to choose between an environment in which the kids were a little shy but produced outstanding academic results or a place where youngsters were more outgoing but far less studious and were randomly flung onto railway tracks from time to time, I know which one I would pick, don't you? Quick! Make your mind up, a train is approaching.

Chapter Six

I cannot stand shopping in Singapore. No, that is wrong. I cannot stand shopping with my girlfriend in Singapore. I spend so much time with her in Orchard Road and Bishan that I am considering taking a sleeping bag with me from now on. You see, like most women, she is a feeler. She simply cannot walk past an unfamiliar product without giving it a quick, discreet fondle. It does not matter what we are looking at, her hands impulsively shoot out to touch that unidentified sitting object. I would not mind but there are parts of my body that remain unidentified but she has never been overcome by an uncontrollable urge to touch them. I have seen her feel the most ridiculous of products ranging from baby clothes to tin openers. The most mystifying part of the process comes after she has given the unfamiliar product a squeeze, which, incidentally, she never has any intention of buying. Seemingly delighted that, for example, a roof rack for a BMW (we do not even have a car) feels exactly how she anticipated, her lips form a tiny, self-satisfied smile as she lets out a little 'hmm'. She can do this all bloody day.

So, after spending the whole day shopping one Sunday, it should come as no surprise that I was not in the best of moods as we queued up at a taxi stand outside Junction 8 shopping centre in Bishan. The sticky humidity that precedes a thunderstorm was not helping matters either. I was perspiring heavily, I had things to prepare for work the next day and the taxi queue did not seem to be going anywhere. There were about six taxis' worth of people in front of us when the most irritating thing happened. A Chinese lad, aged about twenty, swaggered towards the queue with his girlfriend. He was speaking Hokkien extremely loudly into a yellow handphone, throwing in plenty of swear words here and there just to remind his academically-challenged girlfriend how hard he was. As a taxi approached, the pair arrogantly walked to the front of the queue, flagged the taxi down and got in. As the unknowing driver pulled away, the Chinese guy dragged himself away from his phone momentarily to wave at the queue before disappearing into the night.

There were grumbles and disappointed sighs from a few weary shoppers waiting in the queue but I was livid. I had travelled to the other side of the planet to get some peace from these shitheads and I was furious with myself for letting the little prick get away with it. My home town was full of people like this.

I was still fuming when the Indian couple standing behind us walked away. I sympathised with them. They were just as pissed off as we were. When they left the queue, I assumed they had given up trying to get a taxi. Curiously, I watched them plod along Bishan Road. They had walked no more than fifteen metres when they stepped off the kerb and hailed a taxi that was making its way towards the stand. The couple quickly got in, probably hoping they had not been spotted, and the taxi then pulled away sharply. I could not believe it. I had been made to look a fool twice in two minutes. This time something had to be done.

As the taxi crawled up to the stand, I found myself inexplicably running towards it. 'You bastards!' I heard myself shout. 'You fucking little kiasu bastards. Don't pretend you can't see me. There are families waiting to get taxis here, you fucking bastards.'

So there I was in the middle of Bishan Road on a wet Sunday night screaming abuse at a taxi that was fast becoming a twinkling light in the distance. What was I doing? I still cannot explain it rationally. On completing my incoherent tirade of abuse, I turned, delighted with myself, towards the taxi stand. The sight of ten or so stunned shoppers greeted me, all of whom had no idea what to make of my uncontrolled outburst. Sometimes the Dagenham side of me comes racing to the surface because that is the side that stores all the swear words. There is little I can do about it.

Nothing in Singapore brings out that side of me quicker than kiasuism – a paranoid trait that made the Indian couple push in front of families with small children so they could be home ten minutes earlier than everybody else. It was kiasuism, I believe, that made the taxi driver pull over in the first place. He could see the long queue that he was barely fifteen metres from and I am sure he knew what the couple was doing, but he wanted to get his taxi meter running as quickly as possible and he could do it without the hassle of pulling into a taxi stand. Paranoid? I do not think so.

Had that incident occurred during my first week in Singapore, I am fairly certain that Scott and I would have called them 'cheeky bastards' and shrugged off the incident. Having now lived in Singapore for over five years, I experience some form of kiasuism every day. To me, it is the city-state's most negative (and most visible) feature.

In Hokkien, *kiasu* means 'to be scared to fail'. To a certain extent, it can be a positive characteristic in certain spheres of society.

For example, the fear of failing encourages parents to provide the best education possible for their children. But it never stops at this healthy level. Many Singaporeans like immediate, positive results. They cannot wait for things; they must have them now and they must be the first to have them. After all, what is the point of coming second? No one remembers the losers.

So what does all this lead to? Well, the 'Hello Kitty' 2000 phenomenon, of course. This phenomenon was not a national struggle to acquire the rights for a two-party system but rather the Singaporean population's desire to purchase the ugliest set of cat dolls humankind has ever seen.

The sad fact is that the Hello Kitty nightmare started calmly enough. These Japanese midgets had already been on sale in various guises and costumes in Singapore for some time when a fast-food chain announced that it would sell pairs of the dolls wearing different costumes with value meals. But if Hello Kitty products were already available elsewhere, why was there such a massive demand? Ladies and gentlemen, please allow the marketing gurus to step forward and take a well-deserved bow. They ingeniously tapped into the Singaporean psyche – the kiasu 'whatever you have, I must have' syndrome. It was one of the most successfully orchestrated marketing campaigns of recent times.

How did the burger chain pull off this marketing miracle and turn usually sane Singaporeans into cold-blooded, green-eyed Hello Kitty hunters? Simple. It slapped 'limited edition' all over the little felines. Thus creating a wonderfully unique situation for the kiasu consumer. That is, the 'whatever I have, you might not be able to have, ha' syndrome. Now if that is not waving a red rag to a kiasu bull, then I do not know what is. And boy, did many Singaporeans see red.

When the first pair of Hello Kitty dolls went on sale, the country went ballistic and the dolls were sold out within hours. Knowing this, people began to queue the night before the next pair of dolls were due to go on sale. Can you believe it? These people were even shown on the news camping outside various fast-food eateries. I was stunned. Until then, the only society of people I had ever come across that loved queuing was the British. It is one of our national pastimes. My fellow countrymen spend half their lives queuing and they are exceedingly good at it. Try to cut in a queue at the post office in Dagenham and you will be thrown looks that suggest you have just committed murder.

In Singapore, where the lifestyle is so hectic, I was given the impression that its citizens barely have enough time to breathe, let alone the patience to stand and queue. Even in my local bank, there is no need to queue. They employ a wonderful system, whereby you simply take a ticket, sit down in a comfortable chair, read a book and wait for your ticket number to be called. Increasingly, Singapore is becoming a queue-free zone.

So you can imagine how shocked I was when I read about the hordes of people eagerly queuing overnight for a pair of dolls. Many teenagers probably saw camping out as an adventure. And if these youngsters had been the only people involved, I suspect the whole episode would have been a comparatively light-hearted affair. But they were not. The kiasu brigade came in and took over. There were those who queued up to buy more than ten pairs of the dolls, which led to a limit on the number of sets each customer could buy. Then there were those who hired students to queue for them, thus creating the first professional queuers ever employed to purchase a pair of cuddly toys. People were arrested and fined for disorderly behaviour. At Bukit Panjang, stools were thrown at police officers. Others had fights in front of women and children over alleged queue cutting. Consequently, Cisco, a private security firm, was hired to place guards at some of the bigger stores. Finally, several people were injured when a shop window in Bedok shattered under the pressure of too many impatient fuckers leaning on it.

In the end, the fast-food chain placed a full-page advertisement in the national newspapers apologising for the chaos. The burger chain also guaranteed that the last pair of dolls would not be limited and supplies would match demand, thus ensuring the end of both overnight queuing and the Hello Kitty phenomenon in general. Of course, if this strategy had been employed in the first place, none of the above would have happened.

Once the farce had subsided, people were quick to step forward to analyse the incident and try to understand and even justify it. Some claimed impressionable adults and teenagers had simply fallen for a cunning marketing ploy. Others came up with the silly idea that Singaporeans had a penchant for queuing. Believe me, that is a complete falsehood. In a country where its citizens cannot wait three seconds for commuters to alight from a train before getting on, the very idea of standing in a queue for over eight hours would be anathema. No, it all comes down to greed. Pure greed. When those damned cats were stamped 'limited edition', it created a stampede of would-be entrepreneurs. Within days, these characterless toys were being auctioned on local web sites and they were being sold for S$50 or more at flea markets.

One of my closest friends, Victor, admitted that he had queued up for eight hours in Toa Payoh. I almost forgave him when he said he took turns with his fiancée to queue because they were getting married in a few weeks and he wanted a pair of the wedding dolls for good luck. I was none too pleased when he told me that he had managed to sell the other pairs for S$50 a go. This just floored me. The dolls cost about S$10 a pair so he had made S$40 profit on each pair that he had sold after queuing for almost a full working day. The most infuriating part was that Victor knew what he was doing. He said, 'I wanted a set for the wedding. But when I saw how much people were paying for the dolls, I thought "why not?" Everybody was doing it. I saw people being paid to queue. What to do? We love to have something free or be the first to have something.' That is the trouble with greed, it clouds all logic.

However, kiasuism goes way beyond greed. Undoubtedly, it ties in with avarice in the sense that you must be the first to have something whether it is a stuffed cat, a cinema ticket, a lottery ticket or a condominium. Ultimately though, it is a phobia. A terrifying dread of not winning, of coming second and possibly even, and I am going to have to use a rude word here, failing. Singaporeans would rather step into a boxing ring with a pissed off auntie before admitting that they might not have fully succeeded at something. So from the earliest age, they strive to be as efficient and as competent as they possibly can in the area of academic study because that is pretty much all they do in childhood. But then it progresses and becomes all encompassing. Kiasuism spreads rapidly though the brain (and in severe cases down to the anus because that is what badly afflicted victims talk out of) and eats away at you like Parkinson's disease.

My first direct experience of the kiasu syndrome came from listening to Melissa, a former colleague, complaining at work one day. We were all sitting at a table eating lunch when she just launched herself into a frenzy. 'Ooh, I was fuming at the MRT station this morning. I was waiting to get on the train when someone brushed past me and got straight on. The worst part was that there was a mother with her baby in a buggy waiting to get on the train as well but this guy just didn't care. He brushed past her as well. So kiasu.'

After that, I found out what kiasuism meant and began to hunt it down. It can be spotted every day on any transportation system. In a nutshell, people do not wait for you to get off the train before they get on. It is as simple as that. You are invisible. To the kiasu mind, you do not exist; he or she must get on the train as soon as possible. If it means brushing past ten people to do so, so be it.

I have only reacted to it once. Scott and I were alighting from a train at City Hall on our way to watch an S-League football match, when suddenly, thwack! My left shoulder was hit so hard that I bumped into Scott. 'You little prick. Couldn't you see me, you dopey bastard?' And the doors closed. I was angry because it was a young Malay lad who had arrogantly strutted onto the train with his girlfriend the split-second the doors had opened. He was showing off. Scott took no notice, of course; he was too busy giggling. 'You nearly got knocked out by a kid,' he said. So I pushed him down the escalator.

There is simply nothing you can do to stop the impending stampede as the doors of an MRT train open. In my more ludicrous moments, I have tried to devise a human dam, i.e., me, to hold back the tide. However, let me state for the record – I am no Moses. If you gave me a plastic bucket and spade, I reckon I would have a better chance of parting the Red Sea than holding back kiasu commuters. Even if I stand on the markings on the platform floor that show you where you should stand to get on the train and avoid alighting passengers, I can only block one side of queuing passengers so kiasu commuters simply walk around me and cut in from the other side. Believe me, if there is a gap, they will find it.

Then there are the Singaporean bus services.

When I was a kid growing up in the late seventies, there used to be a comedy show on television called *On the Buses*. It was quite funny and well written but it gave me nightmares thanks to Jack the bus conductor. Jack was supposed to be the Juan de Marco of London's bus service and the terror of all female passengers. Yet he must have been the ugliest man on the planet. Painfully thin, he consisted of a cluster of bones all held in place by the belt of his grey skin-tight bus uniform. His long, narrow face suggested he had spent his formative years trapped in a vice. Nevertheless, the scriptwriters seemed oblivious to all of his physical failings and gave him the sort of lines usually reserved for Brad Pitt. In some ways, the fact that the leering, dirty old man (he was in his late forties even then) did not look like Clark Gable made it funnier. However, as a four-year-old boy, he horrified me. When my mother took me shopping, I was afraid of travelling on buses in case Jack the bus conductor pounced. I knew that he would say some of the same lines to my mother and she would laugh and run away and leave me. I did not lose my phobia until *On the Buses* was taken off the air. By then, Jack was nearing retirement and chasing girls was leaving him visibly breathless. And Viagra was still a pipe dream.

My fear of buses returned with a vengeance when I arrived in Singapore. Jack the elderly sex bomb was replaced by 'Skippy the 238 Man', the crazed, hyperactive driver of the number 238 feeder bus service that covers the housing estates of Toa Payoh Lorong 8. I hear that the Singapore Bus Services (SBS) have cloned him countless times to take care of the other feeder services throughout the island. Rumour has it that he was cloned from the DNA of Skippy the kangaroo and mixed with a dollop of kiasuism to produce his unique driving style.

He pulls into the bus stop and you innocently board with your farecard in your left hand and a bag of shopping in the other. Just as you lift your card to slot it into the machine, he pulls away sharply. Suddenly, the bag of shopping has a pull stronger than the tide and you find yourself lying horizontally along the aisle still holding your farecard. It is a nightmare.

No matter who drives the number 238 bus, the methods for getting from A to B are identical. 'Skippy' will pull away from the bus stop as fast as he can and, not forgetting his intensive kiasu training, leaves it until the last possible second before braking. On a regular bus journey, such a technique would be mildly irritating. However, it is positively infuriating on a feeder service where stops can be as little as 200 metres apart. Many passengers refuse to sit down because if they do, they know there is a better than average chance that they will end up sitting on the lap of the person in front.

This erratic driving boils down to kiasuism. In fact, bus travel itself could be a case study. From bus drivers trying to cover small distances at recklessly high speeds to passengers rushing onto the bus to take the seats positioned near the exit door, it is all an upshot of trying to get things done quicker and getting to destinations faster to improve efficiency. By the way, if a picture ever painted a thousand words, it has to be the sight of twenty people sitting on the outside-edge of twenty double seats. Why do people do that? It means that the next poor sod that gets on the bus has to ask someone to move so that he can sit on the other half of the seat. When this happens, the person sitting on the edge of the seat shoots him a look that suggests she would like to kick him between the legs. Then, she sighs emphatically and merely moves her legs to one side, meaning he now has to squeeze past her to sit by the window. In this situation, I have perfected a technique in which I drop a shoulder, swing my rucksack around and deliver a deft blow to the side of the old bat's temple. I have asked many friends why Singaporeans do this as it does not happen in England. Some have suggested that passengers panic that they might miss their stop if the bus gets packed. I find this a dubious theory because, as I am sure you have noticed, kiasu types press the stop button 15 hours before the bus approaches the bus stop. Others believe that travellers want to sit away from the window to avoid the Sun or that they just want the whole damn seat to themselves. I suspect that it is an amalgam of all these theories, with kiasuism lurking in the shadows.

Kiasuism has even led to a bus crashing less than thirty seconds after I had boarded it. Travelling to work one Sunday afternoon after doing some shopping, I got on the number 16 bus opposite Dhoby Ghaut MRT station. Quite typically for a Sunday afternoon, there was heavy traffic and the bus was behind at least four other buses in the bus lane. It was real bumper-to-bumper stuff. The kiasu driver was impatiently revving his engine and edging forward. Looking further down the bus lane, he anticipated that the bus in front would start moving. Only it did not. Nevertheless, the bus I was in did move and we merrily smacked into the back of the bus in front, smashing our windscreen and its rear window. The incident was pathetic really. I had only just collected my farecard from the machine and was walking down the aisle when it happened. Having just left my partner at the bus stop, I could see her through the window laughing hysterically. The passengers all reacted with considerable good humour. Although the woman opposite me was clutching a Bible to her chest, which I thought was a little premature.

Without doubt, kiasuism is everywhere. I have seen, or rather I have heard, people taking handphone calls while sitting on a public toilet, doing bench presses in a gym, attending a wedding ceremony in a church and even teaching secondary school students in a classroom. The strive to be first and the desire not to miss out on anything has become overwhelming.

And in what I believe to be one of the most ironic chains of events in modern Singaporean history, kiasuism was cultivated by the very institution that is now trying in vain to quell it – the government. With legitimate intentions, I think the government unleashed within its people an uncontrollable human vice: greed. Think about it. When Singapore was kicked out of Malaysia in 1965, who could it turn to for help? The British had already screwed up once during World War II when, out of a mixture of ignorance and arrogance, they most kindly stepped aside for the invading Japanese forces. The British returned briefly after the war to top up their fading sun tans and then promptly buggered off again, this time for good. In 1965, Malaysia told Lee Kuan Yew to do the same. So Singaporeans were left with a fledgling government and an unstable economy, which needed to supply everything. With Britain and Malaysia out of the equation, no one was going to give Singaporeans anything. They were going to have to help themselves.

With incredible foresight, Lee Kuan Yew made a speech shortly after Singapore's independence in 1965 in which he predicted the country's transformation into a metropolis. The amazing thing is that against all expectations the government and its people achieved their goal and Singaporeans became one of the most productive labour forces on the planet.

Undoubtedly, such rapid progress is going to get the average man on the street thinking. Even in his wildest dreams, he probably did not expect to achieve so much so soon. Having secured a decent three-roomed flat for his family and a reasonable level of education for his children, he is entitled to assume, therefore, that if he raises his productivity further, the flat could increase to five rooms and his kids might be able to attend university. Inevitably, Singaporeans across the island make similar assumptions and push themselves and their families even harder to improve themselves socially and economically. This is wonderful news for the government as it is a clear popular mandate for its policies. So, in turn, the government makes an effort to increase productivity and efficiency within its spheres of influence, such as the civil service, housing, the national airport, the country's shipping ports and the nation's transportation services. Productivity targets are constantly being set and exceeded in all these areas, bank balances rise and shop tills keep on ringing.

However, when such a socioeconomic phenomenon peaks, two human weaknesses inevitably arise: greed and fear. Unlike the old days of struggle and shared hardship, Singapore has evolved into an individualistic rat race: a materialistic society in which anything is attainable if you work harder than everyone else. Years of being told by parents, teachers and politicians that you must provide for yourself, because no one else will, has moulded the average Singaporean into a kiasu king and transformed my generation into a bunch of greedy bastards. For the sake of economic prosperity, it forsook communal spirit for individual avarice. For laudable political reasons, the government unleashed a social disease that has no cure.

And to satisfy greed, you must maintain efficiency and that is where fear comes in. All over the country, employees live in fear of failing to reach their targets. I saw a sign at Toa Payoh MRT station guaranteeing that 94 per cent of all train services would be on time. This is an astonishingly high figure that helps explain MRT kiasuism on so many different levels. In a way, those annoying passengers who push and shove their way onto the train before others get off have valid reasons for doing so. It is quite simply because that annoying woman on the recorded message is already announcing that the doors are closing three bloody seconds after the doors have opened. It is an insane race against the clock to get on board. I can recall at least two occasions during rush hour when I have travelled with a large group of colleagues and one of the others did not make it onto the train. Both times, we ended up waving goodbye to the one left behind on the platform in the same way that soldiers waved to their loved ones in the old war movies. Why is it such a mad rush? Simple. The guy up front driving the train is shitting his pants that his train may not fall within the 94 per cent band, which would then affect his bonus and put back his flat upgrading by a year. Just like Skippy the 238 Man knows he must complete his designated route within very stringent time limits.

That, for me, is kiasuism. We are all guilty of it. I push past people to get on the train or the bus because I want to get on the damn thing. In those situations, it is a case of kill or be killed. Nevertheless, I really hate myself for doing it. I should know better and so should the Singaporeans who do it. The idea of self-help and pushing oneself to the limit was necessary for the republic to grow during its infancy but it is no longer necessary. The recent currency crisis, if nothing else, should have taught the shallow that there is more to life than greed. Living standards can still be improved without the need to eliminate all competition or to be first all of the time. So if you should find yourself at the end of a long taxi queue one day, waiting behind families and women with bags of shopping, do not be a prick and push in. There really will be another taxi along shortly.

Chapter Seven

My home is surrounded by lunatics. Oh, I do not mean the likes of Hannibal Lecter or my mother but merely the harmless weirdos who seem to frequent my apartment block from time to time, with the explicit intention of affording me as many laughs as possible. It seems these people were placed on Earth for people to laugh at them. It is their mission in life.

And I am delighted to state for the record that living in Housing & Development Board (HDB) apartments in Singapore does provide the observant individual with more than enough nutcases to provide a few giggles. The best part is that they tend to zoom in on the quaint or the unusual, so being Caucasian and extremely tall, I get the lion's share of all the lunatics on my estate.

The first one latched onto me as I got off the number 143 bus at Jalan Toa Payoh one evening. He grunted the strangest greeting. 'Hey, big boy,' he shouted.

Distant memories of Scott and I being drunk in a Leeds gay bar during our university days came flooding back. 'Big boy.' There it was again.

I turned to find a large Chinese man walking just behind me, carrying shopping bags and wearing a huge grin.

'Sorry?' I said.

'Wah, you big boy, ah? So strong. Jim?'

'Who's Jim?'

'No, lah. You go gym to keep fit, is it?'

'Oh, I see. Yeah, a few times a week.' This was a blatant lie. You only need look at me to realise this but I was starting to like the guy. Then came the surreal interrogation.

'Where you stay?'

'Here. Toa Payoh.'

'You on holiday?'

'No, I live here.'

'Which country?'

'Singapore!'

'No, lah. Which country you from?'

'Oh! England.'

'But you so big, you know. How come so big?'

'Er, I play some sports.'

'Oh! I've just bought some fish for dinner. You eat fish?'

'A little.'

'How tall are you? Two metres?'

'No, about 1.92 metres.'

He looked me up and down, unconvinced. 'No lah, you two metres. Which block you stay?'

'Erm, that one over there.' I pointed to the block that faces mine to avoid the possibility of him knocking on my door in the dead of night, holding a measuring tape and ready to prove me wrong.

'Oh, I stay in that block.' Shit, he nodded towards the block that I really do live in.

'So, is your family tall?'

'Quite tall.'

'Yeah, I think so. I'm cooking fish tonight. Where are you going now?'

'Oh, I'm just going over to the shop to buy some groceries and a big gun. Bye.'

I still see the old sod now and again and he always calls out 'big boy', which has caused more than a few startled stares in my general direction. We usually talk about general stuff like my height, the weather, my height, food and my height. Whenever I have caught up with him, he is always on his own and I suspect he lives alone. Nevertheless, the jovial chap never stops smiling and likes nothing more than a brief chat, which is more than can be said for 'Vidal Sassoon'.

I first came across Vidal in a lift one morning, about three months after I had moved in. Wearing an old, faded samfoo, Vidal was already in the lift when I got in on the fifth floor. She then proceeded to stare up at me non-stop all the way down to the ground floor. That is only five floors, I hear you cry. Well, ask the person next to you to stare into your face for the next five seconds. It becomes just a trifle disconcerting, doesn't it? Stepping out of the lift, Vidal turned to stare a little longer, almost blocking my path. I had to step around the old woman to get past her or I suspect we would still be there.

The weirdest thing about Vidal is that she is everywhere. Wearing the same worn-out clothes and dirty flip-flops, I have seen her sitting at the void deck in the HDB estate, shuffling past the local coffee shop, strolling through Toa Payoh Central and even lurking at the end of Balestier Road, which is some two kilometres away. On each occasion, she always finds time to stop and stare at me with that same weary, expressionless face. It is quite chilling.

All of that is nothing compared to the most shocking encounter that I have had with Vidal, an incident that terrified me to my very soul. One evening, I was reading the paper at the table in my living room when my girlfriend screamed. Looking up, I was greeted by the sight of Vidal's little head peering through the door grille and into my living room.

Like most Singaporeans, I often leave the front door open and keep the door grille locked to improve air circulation and reduce stuffiness. People do pass along the common corridor outside but they usually mind their own business. I certainly did not plan for the door grille to become an observation post for loopy old women.

Momentarily, my girlfriend and I sat in stunned silence, as you do when a seventy-year-old woman stares at you sitting in your own living room. Luckily, she had only caught me performing the innocent act of reading the newspaper. I have the socially inept habit of scratching things that itch and it could have become quite a testing situation if I had been caught red-handed.

The problem was that Vidal did not say anything. She just stared and I knew for a fact that she either did not understand English or, at least, had problems interpreting it. Whatever sentence I threw at her, her brain would probably translate it to mean 'Hello, auntie. Please could you gawp at me for a little while longer because I'm really enjoying it.'

After about twenty seconds of suffering intense staring, I could see my girlfriend looking at me, motioning that it was time for me to do something.

'Hello, auntie. Ni hao ma?' My pathetic attempt to win her over by asking how she was in Mandarin caused absolutely no reaction.

'Okay, auntie. I think that's enough peeping for one day. Off you go. Bye.' I tried to shoo her away with my hand but that only titillated her. She then started to smirk at my partner.

'For fuck's sake, Neil. Get rid of her, will you? She's grinning at me now,' my girlfriend complained.

'Auntie, time to go. No more looking, understand? Go away.' More staring and more smirking. 'Enough now. Please go. Bye.'

Left with the distinct possibility of her standing there all night, I got up, smiled at her and closed the door. Walking back to the table, I was struck by the horrifying thought of my partner leaving for work the next morning and being greeted by a short, smirking auntie. The shock would probably have killed them both. I went back to the door and looked through the peephole to see if she was still there but the old bat had moved on to her next haunt. She still passes along the corridor occasionally but she merely turns her head and looks in briefly, she does not actually stop now.

But here is the remarkable thing. Although Vidal is always wearing the same tatty samfoo and the same old battered flip-flops, she has the smartest hairstyle. I have spotted her on my way to work in the morning and again late at night when I am returning home and she always looks as though she has just stepped out of a salon. I have pointed her out to Singaporean friends and they agree that Vidal (now you know why I call her this) is a bizarre phenomenon who defies all logical explanation. After all, how do you explain a woman who wears the same clothes every day, has the brains of a rocking horse, yet wears her hair like Cameron Diaz?

Nevertheless, even Vidal pales in comparison to 'bra lady', who, would you believe, also lives in my apartment block. Bra lady makes Vidal look like a professor in nuclear physics. She is so insane that I am convinced the asylum lets her out on day release just to provide the local community with a little comic relief.

Like me, bra lady's major hobby is travel, which she vigorously pursues in her spare time. However, like most people, I like to explore new countries and cultures whereas she likes to explore lifts. To be more specific, she likes to explore and travel in the lifts in my block throughout the whole bloody day. I think she believes that she performs the unofficial, unpaid duties of a lift attendant on behalf of the HDB.

I vividly recall the first time I caught her in action. After pressing the button on the fifth floor, my partner and I watched the lift descend from the twelfth floor, stopping at every floor along the way before reaching ours. Mildly irritated at the delay, we got into the lift to find that the only other person in the lift was bra lady. Why did I christen her bra lady? Because she was performing her lift attendant duties while wearing her bra *over* her clothes. As women are more observant in these situations, my partner was the first to spot the large pink bra over bra lady's shirt. My partner then elbowed me in the rib cage to get my attention. Trying to prevent myself from roaring with laughter, I distracted myself by approaching the lift panel to press the ground floor button. But, silly me, I had no need to fear because bra lady had already kindly pressed the button. In fact, she had courteously pressed every button on the panel, yet she did not alight at any of the floors and no one else got in.

When we reached the ground floor, my girlfriend got out but I paused briefly to watch bra lady as she meticulously performed her professional duties of pressing every button on the panel from one to twelve. Staring straight ahead at all times and never once looking in our general direction, bra lady closed the doors of the lift and she began yet another ascent.

I am fortunate enough to encounter cuckoos like bra lady, Vidal Sassoon and big boy on a fairly regular basis because I live in an HDB apartment block in Singapore. These government-built concrete, rectangular blocks, so often criticised by ignorant Western visitors, house all kinds of weird and wonderful people. In fact, by 1998, the HDB had built 833,814 units, housing 2,702,000 people – a figure that accounts for 86 per cent of the country's population. I have lived in various HDB apartments for over four years now and I would not live anywhere else. Condominiums might provide swimming pools, saunas, barbecue pits and tennis courts, and I would be lying if I said I would not like having such facilities at the bottom of my block, but they lack a certain vibrancy that comes with living in HDB flats.

Just a few weeks ago, a bunch of lower secondary schoolboys were kicking a ball around the void deck of my block. Now this is against the law and signs are plastered all around the void decks clearly stating that all ball games are prohibited. After all, these and other young lads could chip the paint, dirty the walls and cause considerable noise pollution for the residents living above. So being an upstanding young fellow of the HDB community, what did I do? I asked to join in, of course. We all had a great laugh. Then I received two major shocks. First, I found out that one of the Chinese lads was, like me, a West Ham United supporter and had been all his life. In a country where kiasuism prevails, Singaporeans have a tendency to follow winners like Manchester United, Liverpool or Arsenal. Therefore, I had never met a Singaporean who supported my East London team. The boy then floored me again by giving me a golden West Ham United sticker badge as a gift. The sticker badge now sits proudly on the side of my computer monitor. And as I stare at it now, it reminds me of the warmth, friendliness and safety that comes with living in an HDB flat. These feelings could not be extended back to England.

In my second year at Manchester University, Elizabeth, one of the girls I was sharing a house with, brought a guy she had met at a bar back home with her. If she had walked through the door with a so-called HDB heartlander, I would have relaxed but the guy was a violent local, who, when informed by my ever-so-subtle housemate that she did not want to sleep with him after all, promptly went mental. He took half a crate of beer (he had drunk the other half) and smashed it around the living room. He then proceeded towards the front door where he was met by a half-asleep Reza, our other housemate. Now Reza, who is half-Indian, half-Polish and born and raised in Lancashire, has this unshakable habit of being in the wrong place at the wrong time. That night was no exception. Taking a nap, he was woken up by the slightly odd sound of beer cans being smashed outside his bedroom. Rousing himself, he opened his bedroom door to find a psychopath redecorating our hallway with beer. Equally shocked by the presence of a half-Polish, half-Indian man dressed in pyjamas, the lunatic head-butted Reza before smashing his way out of the house. We later heard that the Mancunian lunatic lived nearby. Such neighbourly behaviour puts Vidal Sassoon's peeping Tom exploits into perspective.

It also helps illustrate some of the differences between the housing environment that I left behind and the one that I am a part of today. Here, Singaporean children play football below my HDB block and I join in. When I was living in Dagenham, children amused themselves by lighting fires outside the doctor's surgery located opposite my mother's house. Neighbours, including my mother, would tell them to pack it in or they would call the police. They were usually told to 'fuck off'. Quite a contrast.

Since its inception in 1960, the Housing & Development Board has, without doubt, done a remarkable job of building not only houses for its people but also creating a clean and safe environment for its residents. In 2000, Singapore had a population of 4.1 million, creating a population density of 5,900 per square kilometre. In the United States, the population density is just 29 per sq. km. In my country, it is 238 per sq. km. So we are talking about a lot of Singaporeans living in a very small space.

After writing a thesis on municipal housing at university, I find the HDB's accomplishments astounding. More so when you consider the state of Singapore in 1960. Then, wooden houses built on stilts formed *kampungs*, or villages. Although these kampungs fostered a sense of community, similar to the London slums at the end of the nineteenth century, the homes themselves could be hazardous. In May 1961, for instance, a fire at Bukit Ho Swee left around 16,000 people homeless. Remarkably though, the HDB had managed to build flats for all these people by February 1962. By the 1970s, the HDB had pretty much solved the nation's housing problems. They may not look pretty but, like my old housing estate in Dagenham, HDB apartments put a modern roof over the heads of its people.

A modern house, however, does not necessarily make for a home. When I studied my own housing estate, I discovered that its newcomers often returned to their London slums because they missed being part of a close-knit community. The Singaporean government is faced with that same problem today.

Residents often lament the loss of the kampung collective spirit that died when their wooden homes were bulldozed. My friends are forever telling me stories about how they shared cups of sugar with neighbours and how all the children in the kampung played together, went to school together and ate together. Nowadays, people tend to care only about family members living under the same roof. The grille to their HDB unit is locked and they close themselves off from their neighbours. They will exchange pleasantries in the hallway but that is about as far as it goes. If you walk along the void deck of any HDB block, the sight of old-timers sitting and chatting will invariably confront you. They still share that kampung bond. With the younger, more affluent generations now living in self-contained units, this bond no longer exists. The nature of one's improved environment has allowed individualism to supersede collectivism.

Of course, it is a social phenomenon that is not unique to Singapore. Even after my housing estate was built in the 1920s, its inhabitants valiantly tried to reestablish their old East London cockney communities. Back garden fences were kept low and neighbours would often chat across them. I once saw my mother hold a three-way conversation with two neighbours, each of whom lived five houses down from my mother's in opposite directions.

Moreover, our low back fence allowed my mother to show off her gymnastic abilities. Early one morning, she was hanging out some washing when she saw Charlie, our next-door neighbour, lying face down on the path in his back garden. Charlie was a lovely old man who dressed immaculately and never complained, even though I must have climbed over his fence more times than a cat burglar to retrieve my football.

On that terrible day, my mother sprang into action. She claims that she threw the washing down, hitched up her skirt and, with no concern for her own safety, jumped straight over the fence and went to Charlie's aid. After examining him, she pronounced him dead at the scene.

Charlie's death illustrates the sad social phenomenon that plagues England and, increasingly, Singapore. Had he died today, my mother would not have noticed. Our back garden now has a two-metre-high fence running all the way round it, as do most of the other houses in my street. Man has always been entitled to his castle but now he wants to build a moat around it.

Singapore is faced with the same problem. In 1964, the HDB launched the Home Ownership Scheme and thousands of Singaporeans bought their apartment units at affordable prices. Today, a staggeringly high 92 per cent of all public flats on the island are owner-occupied. Of course, the logic behind home ownership is politically sound. A resident will look after his home if it is his. However, when he closes the door to the outside world, he immediately severs those kampung bonds. The *Straits Times* often runs stories of elderly HDB residents lying dead at home for several days. In a non-welfare society that already encourages self-help in the workplace, such individualism cannot be helpful in the long run and the government knows this. Thus, it has employed various strategies, such as the ongoing upgrading programmes, to reignite that sense of togetherness within the HDB estates. These upgrading programmes aim to give older HDB estates, like Toa Payoh, a well-deserved face lift with an added room here and a lick of paint there.

My apartment block was recently upgraded and it proved to be an awful experience. Apart from being woken by the joyous sounds of pneumatic drills and sledge hammers every morning, I also enjoyed the added luxury of having the entire rat population of Toa Payoh pack its suitcases and move to the bottom of my block. I felt like I was sharing the apartment with the Stuart Little family. I would come home every night, look down at the building site below and play 'spot the rat'. My record, and I am not joking, was eleven. The average person would probably shrug off such a statistic but I happen to have a terrifying phobia of all things rodent. On many a dark night, Toa Payoh residents have been greeted by the site of a blurred Caucasian sprinting past them screaming, 'It's a fucking *big* rat!' The building site is now a beautiful garden and the rodents have all moved off to the upgrading project across the road.

More seriously, the programmes have also made architectural attempts to bring the residents together again. Apartment blocks are now linked by sheltered walkways, more communal areas with tables and chairs have been built on the void decks and in the gardens while playgrounds have been built in the hope that more children and their parents will come together. Will these improvements work in the long run? Probably not. It is still largely the elderly who sit and chat on the void decks, although more kids play together in the playgrounds, which is encouraging news. The younger generations are, of course, at work chasing the dollar so the communal areas remain, by and large, deserted.

Apart from the upgrading programmes, in Toa Payoh alone there is a small public park, a modern library next to a new public amphitheatre, a swimming complex, a cinema and coffee shops all over the place. In fact, in every corner of Toa Payoh, there are discernible attempts by the local town council to bring its people together. Yet the town centre remains a brain-numbing blur of people scurrying to the bank, the post office or the supermarket before rushing back to their apartments.

Ironically, the only thing that does seem to bring HDB neighbours together is a good old-fashioned crime. As soon as a police siren is heard screaming outside your block, doors and front grilles are opened and before you can say *'kaypoh'*, the corridor is brimming with eagle-eyed neighbours.

About a month after we moved into our flat, my girlfriend and I heard the sound of screeching brakes and shouting voices below so we went out to look. By the time I had opened the front grille, about twenty residents were already standing outside gossiping among themselves. Within five minutes, we had met and chatted with more of our neighbours than we had in the whole of the first month. I was convinced that they all had access to a police radio because they knew everything. They explained that a woman had stabbed her husband in an argument, then run out of the house and was now walking the streets, dazed and wielding a bloodstained knife. This all sounded a little melodramatic to me but who was I to argue with the people in the know? The incident lasted about an hour and by the end of it, we had given some clothes to one neighbour for her niece and a woman at the end of the corridor wondered if we had ever considered Buddhism.

The whole episode would not have happened in England. Fear would have kept everybody's doors firmly closed. I remember a police van pulling up outside my friend's house one night. Without pulling back the curtains, we peered through a tiny crack to see what was going on. Four policemen got out of the van and, after some running and lots of swearing, they arrested two brothers. The interesting thing to note is that not a single soul came out to witness what was quite a unique event. No one wanted to get involved for fear of recrimination. After all, what if the two brothers spotted you? They would assume that you had grassed them up to the police.

When I recall these incidents, I really do appreciate Singapore, its people and the benefits of living in an HDB block. In terms of architectural stature, the apartments may not be up there with New

York's Chrysler Building and, in an ideal world, I would prefer Singaporean children to have a garden to play in. However, when you have a population density of 5,900 per sq. km, what else can you do? The HDB makes the best of a difficult situation, even if it does weaken that wonderful kampung spirit.

And I am proud to live in Toa Payoh, Singapore's second satellite town, complete with educational, vocational and recreational facilities. To me, it is the Dagenham of Singapore and I have a strong attachment to both the place and its people. I love playing football with the young lads at the bottom of my block. It may be technically illegal but sod it. Build more football pitches and sports fields for the children and fewer condominiums and golf courses and we will stop playing on the void decks. I have fun watching the old-timers gamble, sorry, I mean play Chinese checkers on the void decks. I like feeding the turtles at Toa Payoh Park and eating homemade chicken and mushroom pies in the town centre on Sunday mornings. I could go on forever but I think you get the general idea. Besides I must dash – Vidal Sassoon is at the door.

Chapter Eight

Every now and again, we find ourselves privy to some magnificent spectacle or event that serves to reaffirm our humble place in the great state of nature. It could be any kind of incident, such as an earthquake, a hurricane or even the ever-growing hole in the ozone layer, that reminds us that there is something bigger and greater than humankind at work. For me, there have been two spiritual awakenings in my life that have confirmed this.

The first came at the Singapore Zoological Gardens, where I was lucky enough to witness two giant tortoises mate. It took a whole five minutes for the male to muster the energy to climb on top of the female. Once there, let's just say, I hope for the female's sake the boat was of sufficient size because there was absolutely no motion in the ocean. If the subdued mating couple had died during intercourse, no one would have noticed. Nonetheless, they saw it through as do all tortoises around the world at some point. It then struck me how powerful nature is. Here is an animal that walks like it is treading water, carries its HDB flat on its back and makes love to a soldier's helmet, yet nature compels it to get the job done.

Thinking nature could not possibly astound me again, it presented me with the Grand Canyon one fine Summer morning.

Standing on the edge and peering down at Nature's craftsmanship, I realised conclusively that humankind would never be able to compete on equal terms. Nature constructed the Grand Canyon – I cannot even build things with Lego bricks. Without a doubt, I have never seen any landmark that surpassed the Canyon in its magnitude. It does nothing but impress you.

Unless, of course, you are one of the Singaporeans with whom my partner and I went on an American tour. They actually gave the impression that the whole Grand Canyon sightseeing trip was just one giant bore. They complained about the length of the journey from our hotel in Las Vegas to the Canyon. It appeared that due to their insular narrow-mindedness, they had assumed that the United States was like Singapore, where it is a case of turn left and there is Orchard Road or turn right and there is Raffles Place. They could not understand why the same geographical principles did not apply in the United States. You know, turn left and look, there is Disneyland or turn right and there is the Las Vegas strip.

As we were being thrown around the bus, I heard one guy say to our tour guide, 'Edward, how long will this take? I want to get back to the casino.'

My girlfriend and I looked at each other in disbelief. We had not even arrived at probably one of the most visually-arresting sites on the planet and one of our travelling companions was already saying that he wanted to go back to the casino.

I was convinced that once all the chattering Singaporeans stepped off the bus, the sheer magnitude of the Canyon would shut them up and the silent chasm would swallow any insipid kiasu comments. I was only half-right. The kids on the tour were mesmerised for about the first five minutes, which was to be expected. After a few genuine wide-eyed 'wows', there is only so much a primary school child can do with a view. Then I heard it. The gambling man, who inexplicably wore a blue mackintosh raincoat throughout the tour, even in Nevada, rushed over to his wife and said, 'Quick! Finish taking your photos and I'll ask Edward if we can go back to Las Vegas now.'

It had taken us three hours to get to the Canyon and this guy wanted to leave after fifteen minutes. As there was a general consensus from the rest of the group that they had seen enough, we left. Ever since I had seen the breathtaking, post-apocalyptic *Planet of the Apes*, I knew I would visit the Grand Canyon. And I did, for fifteen minutes.

Looking back, I should have known what kind of holiday it was going to be.

When I booked the West Coast package tour, the agent said, 'You do know that it is a Singaporean tour, don't you?'

Puzzled, I replied, 'You mean to say this isn't the Mongolian tour? Because I was told that it wouldn't be a problem getting two seats with the Mongolian tour.'

He stared at me blankly before reminding me that there was an orientation meeting on Friday.

When we arrived for the orientation fashionably late, my fears that this was not going to be an ordinary holiday were realised. As we entered the room, the guide stopped speaking and the whole tour party turned to stare at us. Had the late John F. Kennedy himself walked in, I do not think they could have conjured a more shocked reaction.

Breaking the deafening silence, the guide asked, 'Can we help you?'

'We've come for the meeting about the U.S. trip,' I replied.

'Are you with this group? Do you have your receipts with you?' After I showed the guide our receipts, he stopped asking questions and introduced himself as Edward. Then it dawned on me. We stood out like the white ball on a snooker table. Not only were we the only Caucasians in a group of about twenty-five but we were also the only non-Chinese. At the time, I put it down to coincidence and thought no more about it. That was a bad move.

Edward went through the basics, discussing things like departure times, the time differences and changing currency. I have to confess that I found the talk informative and I found myself asking one or two questions. I hoped they were rational and sensible because many of the other questions were not. The first came from one woman who seemed to be on a mission in life to redefine the word 'stupid'.

She was a rather petite lady, whom the late Barbara Cartland would have probably called buxom. She had a round face that she chose to accentuate by wearing too much rouge on her cheeks. From a distance, she looked like a strawberry. No, that is not true. She looked like a strawberry in tacky sunglasses. She wore those awful black ones that have gold sovereigns embedded along each of the arms. To the average person, these sunglasses say 'Here is a moron who wants you to know she's paid a lot of money for a pair of sunglasses that look about as attractive as the cheap ones in a night market.' However, to lamebrains like our 'strawberry' friend, these glasses represent the height of good taste. Consequently, she wore them everywhere. In the hotel lobby, on the shaded coach and even on the Terminator 3-D attraction in Universal Studios, which was pitch black! In fact, I think it was the combination of her silly sunglasses, her designer handbag with the awful gold chain handle and her round, red face that made a few American teenagers laugh at her. In these situations, I would have pitied 'strawberry' until she reminded me what a kiasu bitch she really was.

The first time she obliged was in the orientation meeting. Edward was explaining about our accommodation in each of the cities we were visiting when she piped up. 'Edward, why aren't we staying in five-star hotels all the way?'

The room fell quiet. The whole package with flights, hotels, transfers, theme parks and some meals was just over S$2,000. Return flights to the West Coast on Singapore Airlines (our airline for the tour) during peak season usually cost around S$1,400. Therefore, you do not need a calculator to work out that poor old Edward, who took care of hotel bookings, transfers and so forth, had to make S$600 go a very long way. He explained, rather patiently, that all the hotels had three stars and the Holiday Inn in San Francisco had four stars. As far as I am concerned, all the hotels were more than sufficient. But once strawberry had set the ball rolling, all the stupid questions came gushing forth as Edward struggled to hold back the kiasu tide. Blue mac, the gambling man, asked if we could extend our stay in Las Vegas. No, we could not because we were on a tight schedule came the courteous reply. No, we could not because this was a family tour so the selfish arsehole would have to play blackjack with himself would have been my reply.

However, if one topic dominated the tour, it would have to be food. From the orientation through Los Angeles, Las Vegas, Arizona and even San Francisco, the subject of cuisine was never far from my travelling gang's lips. It came up on our first night in Anaheim, Los Angeles. We went to what must have been the cheapest looking Chinese restaurant in Los Angeles. The food was tasty and plentiful, though it did seem somewhat surreal eating Chinese food on my first night in the United States. I felt, at the very least, that we should have been eating ribs or hot dogs and a big slab of mom's homemade blueberry pie. It seemed my companions did not agree.

We began chatting with a young couple who were on their honeymoon. They were pleasant company and we ended up spending a bit of time with them. Yet the guy said the strangest thing. I asked him what he thought of America so far, a crazy question I will readily admit because we had only been in the place for about four hours and they had all been spent in Anaheim, so they hardly counted. And he replied, 'I preferred Europe. It's got all the history, great buildings and everywhere is different.' He paused and then added, 'The food was better there, too.'

Now this startled me a little as he had only had one meal and that was Chinese so he had nothing to compare the European cuisines with. Somewhat stumped, I asked, 'Do you mean all the different Italian and French dishes?' Notice I did not mention English food. I did not want to destroy my credibility after one conversation.

'No, I mean the Chinese food was better.'

'The Chinese food? Where?' I asked incredulously.

'Well, all over really. But I remember a great restaurant in Italy.' And his wife nodded in agreement.

It was the first time that I had ever seen two Singaporeans fall into self-parody so easily. Italy is famous throughout the world for its spaghetti bolognaise, lasagne, cannelloni and its 101 different varieties of pizza. I do not profess to be a food expert. Having grown up on my mother's cooking I cannot be but even I wanted to laugh at this guy. I mean, he was excited about a place that was over 10,000 km away because it had restaurants that served the kind of dishes he could get at any hawker centre in Singapore for S$3.

Once we had broached the subject of food, the floodgates opened. Everyone on our table suddenly perked up, even strawberry, who, up until this point, had been stuffing her face with spoonfuls of sweet and sour pork. Her husband began to talk to the newlyweds about the best Chinese restaurants in Singapore. Eager to bring us into the conversation, he asked my partner and me if we had eaten Chinese food before. So I said, 'Funnily enough, no. Despite their exorbitant prices, we've eaten hamburgers every fucking day for the last three years. Hence the greasy skin, the huge waistline and my partner's habit of mooing when she's around grass. Quite honestly, we wouldn't be able to tell a stick of satay from a chopstick. Both of which I intend to insert up your rectum once I've managed to dislodge them from your wife's prodigious mouth.'

Indeed, this question always floors me. Not because people ask if I have had Chinese food before but because they do not ask me if I have had Chinese food in Singapore before? They cannot possibly assume that in twenty-odd years I have never eaten a Chinese meal in England. Singaporeans must know that London is generously sprinkled with hundreds of Chinese food outlets. Those who have visited England have probably dined at most of them as part of their effort to eat their way around all the Chinese restaurants in the world. It is sad really.

However, it is not as sad as how I felt on my first night in the United States after having listened to my companions discuss where to get the best *chendol* on a tiny island that was on the other side of the globe. This was America. We should have been talking about where we were going over the next few days and what were the best rides for the kids in Knott's Berry Farm Theme Park. Would there be time to stop in Beverly Hills to buy strawberry a more subtle pair of sunglasses? You know, holiday-type stuff.

Towards the end of the trip, as we made our way from Las Vegas to San Francisco, food reared its ugly head once again. Edward was describing our next hotel, the Holiday Inn, when strawberry decided to take a stand. 'Edward, no more Western-style breakfasts, eh?'

'No, it's okay,' Edward replied. 'I've managed to secure porridge for everybody. It will be brought to your room at 7 a.m. sharp.'

'Good, I can't take any more of that Western shit.'

And that was it. I refused to speak to the ignorant bitch for the rest of the holiday. It was only my sensible partner who prevented me from calling everybody on the bus a bunch of wankers. I mean, that comment really was a bridge too far. The selfish *tai tai* was so immeasurably stupid that she could not see that she might have seriously offended two Westerners sitting opposite her. Just humour me for a few seconds if you will. Imagine you are sitting at home with friends enjoying a meal. I walk in, point to your food and say, 'I can't take any more of your Asian shit.' Would you react? We are only human after all. And remember, it is not as if strawberry was in an Asian country. She was in a country where you cannot assume that Chinese porridge will be on the menu every morning, even though it had been for most of the tour thanks to Edward's efforts.

I had always believed that the whole point of travelling was to do the 'When in Rome' bit. With regard to the Singaporeans I went to the United States with, it was a case of 'When in Rome, do as the Singaporeans do'. The Singaporean deputy prime minister Lee Hsien Loong recently said, quite seriously, that Singaporeans can always be spotted overseas. I could not agree more with the chap.

Anyway, I was still seething over the 'Western shit' comment and the compulsory Chinese porridge so I had a quiet word with our beleaguered tour guide. 'Edward, I've got to say something about this porridge arrangement.'

'What's the problem?'

'Well, although I really like Chinese food proved by the fact that I've eaten nothing else all week, I don't really like porridge.'

'That could be a bit tricky, Neil.'

I could feel my anger rising. 'How can it be tricky, Edward? This is America, not Singapore or China or even Asia. All I want to do is to eat the food of the country I am visiting.' I was getting a little sarcastic, which I later regretted, but Edward was sympathetic and when he was one-on-one he was brutally honest, something I respected.

He said, 'Look, people want to eat Chinese food on these tours, which is good for them and good for me because it's cheap. I've been here many times and I know some great places to eat both Chinese and Western food but my guests are happy with Chinese food. Besides, we don't get ang mohs on the trip.'

This last part surprised me. 'Why not?'

'This is a Chinese tour.'

'It's a what?'

'A Chinese tour. We specialise in Chinese tours.'

That explained why there were no Malays or Indians on the trip. But I was still puzzled. 'But you advertised in the *Straits Times*. It's an English newspaper. There was nothing to say Chinese only. What if a Malay family came into the shop? Would you turn them away?'

'No, of course not. But they tend to have their own operators and the Chinese usually come with us. That's why I was surprised to see you at the orientation. But I'll try to organise a different breakfast for you.'

To be fair to the man, he did. He gave us the dollar equivalent in cash. So we slept in, had an early lunch at the famous Pier 39 and watched the sea lions sunbathe in the Bay before visiting the infamous Alcatraz prison. I was hoping to leave strawberry there but she did not go. Her family went with the rest of the tour group to San Francisco's famous Chinatown for, and I am not making this up, a meal at one of its fancy restaurants. It was such a shame because I knew that all the young lads on the trip really wanted to go to Alcatraz. When we met up with them later, they bombarded us with questions about 'The Rock' and all its famous inhabitants. I mean, if you were a fifteen-year-old Singaporean and you had a choice of windowshopping in Chinatown or seeing where Al Capone was incarcerated, which attraction would you choose?

I sympathised with the young lads because I have been in exactly the same predicament. When I was seventeen, my father took my sister and me to the Spanish island of Tenerife, which is the British equivalent of Bintan. It is cheap, sunny, full of beaches, and foreigners have overrun the place. Being young and inquisitive, I wanted to explore the island. Despite the fact that mass tourism has transformed the place into a tacky resort, Tenerife is dominated by a natural wonder – the volcanic mountain, Pico de Teide. Moreover, Franco met his officers on the island in 1936 to plan the nationalist rebellion that sparked the Spanish Civil War, so the island had some history. Did I get to explore any of this? Of course not. For two weeks, I spent my days by the swimming pool, doing my bit to help turn us all into the prune family, and I spent my nights in the bar, tediously watching my father work his way towards liver failure. In short, my father transported his England of beer, burgers and football and replanted it temporarily in Tenerife.

By the end of the holiday, he knew no more about Tenerife than he did when he first arrived on the island but he had swallowed a hell of a lot of beer. Similarly, the Singaporeans with whom I went to America consumed a great deal of Chinese food. In both cases, the bored children had no choice but to sit and watch.

The person in the middle of all this was poor old Edward, the tour guide. At the start of the trip, he looked immaculate. By the time we had reached San Francisco almost two weeks later, it was becoming increasingly difficult to distinguish him from the homeless guys dotted all over California.

Undoubtedly, the stresses of the job made the chap a character. Always fearful of losing one of the party, which I am sure must be any tour guide's nightmare, Edward always made sure he was easily identifiable. Apart from wearing bright pink shirts, he spent his time in the land of the free imitating the Statue of Liberty. No matter where I went, if I looked up at any given time of the day, I would invariably spot a pink Edward twenty metres in front, holding a map in his raised right arm. He always held a map and we always seemed to be chasing after him.

When we went to Universal Studios, we had from 9 a.m. to 4 p.m. to look around. Even though it was one of the busiest months of the year, we saw absolutely everything. From the Back to the Future ride to the studio tour, he somehow managed to squeeze it all in. At times, the group actually ran from one attraction to another. Just picture it. Twenty-five Chinese and two Caucasians all sprinting after a pink Chinese Statue of Liberty. I was pleased to go on the Jurassic Park water ride just to rest for three minutes. But like I say, by 4 p.m., we had seen and done everything. So I have to admit that kiasuism can really come in handy sometimes, especially if you are in an American theme park.

Sometimes, however, it does not. For months, my girlfriend had been driving me mad about Disneyland. Ever since she had watched *Mary Poppins* as a small girl, she has believed in flying umbrellas, talking penguins and nannies who break into song every time their charges misbehave. Consequently, I was fully prepared for the fact that she was going to be insufferable for the entire day. However, spending 12 hours with her inside the Magic Kingdom was nothing compared to spending just over 12 minutes with the kiasu gang outside its entrance. Poor Edward was bombarded with trivial questions.

Strawberry asked, 'Will my children be safe here?'

'No! The "double M" mouse family owns the place and runs a protection racket.'

'Will you be waiting for us when the theme park closes?'

'No, I've left you in the capable hands of a local triad gang.'

'Do we have to stay here all day?'

'No, blue mac, you can leave whenever you want but there are no casinos nearby so you'll just have to play with the traffic.'

Many other pointless questions were asked but the Pulitzer Prize went, rather surprisingly, to strawberry's husband. He said, 'Look at the long queues. Can't you do anything about the queues, Edward? We are part of a large tour.'

This insane request was then followed by a chorus of 'wah, so many people', 'must queue so long' and 'how to get on all the rides in one day?'

Edward promptly lost it. When we reached the counter, he steamed into the young American girl. He complained about having to wait in a long queue even though we already had tickets as we were a group party. Before the poor girl had a chance to respond, irate members of my tour suddenly surrounded the counter, all of whom were bitching to Edward or to the girl or scrambling for free maps. Naturally, blue mac was at the front rudely informing the girl that the theme park should implement a more efficient queuing system. His smugness suggested genuine self-satisfaction for 'educating' this girl, as he had probably done countless times to the waitress at his local country club. But this was America and the delightfully filthy look from the girl suggested that the prick could go fuck himself.

Meanwhile, the other Singaporeans in the group were greedily grabbing extra maps from the counter even though they had all been given a map with their ticket. The girl behind the counter had had enough. 'Look, can you just take one map each, please?' she said irritably but with remarkable self-restraint.

Edward came back to the counter and surpassed himself. 'I need some more maps. Some of my group say they don't have a map.'

'Yes they do, sir. I gave a map to each and every one of them.'

'Well, I need some more,' retorted Edward. I could hear people behind muttering disapprovingly.

'But I gave a map to everyone along with their ticket.'

'I need some more.'

'Oh, for Christ's sake. Take these.' She virtually threw three maps at Edward.

'That's not enough,' he said and then he leant over the counter, grabbed a handful and walked off.

'What are you doing?' the girl shouted but it was too late. Edward was already dishing them out.

When we caught up with the others, they were still bitching about the 'so rude' girl at the counter. Meanwhile, blue mac was telling Edward, who must have been to Disneyland at least twenty times, the best route around the theme park. I had already told Edward that we were more than happy to spend a long day completely lost in the Magic Kingdom so we went off to find the Indiana Jones ride.

As our monumental vacation reached its last leg in San Francisco, I was really pining for Singapore. I missed its safety. Having lived in Singapore for a couple of years now, even I had begun to take its security for granted. So there is nothing like a little bit of Californian poverty to bring you back to your senses. In Chinatown in Los Angeles, I saw an elderly black woman urinating in the street in the middle of the day. Obviously homeless, her clothes were ripped and torn and the poor woman was filthy. Being less than five metres away, we could see everything and she could see us. To calm my startled partner, I tried to revert to the old streetwise Neil of Dagenham, telling her that it was no big deal and that there was poverty in all the major cities of the world. I knew I sounded false and she knew it too. I had been conditioned by Singaporean safety and my words had a hollow ring to them. I was repulsed by the terrible hardship and I did not want to be there either.

Similarly in San Francisco, there were homeless people everywhere and it was tragic. They would beg openly for money and some even pursued us down the street. I hated myself for staying at a four-star hotel while these people slept on benches less than fifty metres away. I felt so ashamed for deliberately avoiding encounters with people who had a social background not a million miles away from mine. In fact, I probably had more in common with these people than I did with many of the group I was travelling with.

This was the other reason why I was homesick for Singapore. I was fed up with the Singaporeans with whom I was travelling. The whole rigmarole of taking photographs was driving me crazy by the time we had reached San Francisco. I seriously wondered if the whole point of them coming on this trip was to take as many photos as possible to prove that they had been there. I can think of no other rationale for my tour party's behaviour.

When Edward took us to a hilly peak that spoilt us with panoramic views of the San Fransisco Bay, it was unquestionably cold. However, I had a quick look around as I thought that I may never go back there, whereas my companions dashed off the heated coach simultaneously, clicked their cameras and then dived back on the bus again. It then occurred to me that they had performed the same ritual throughout the entire tour. At the Hollywood Bowl, where strawberry had famously wondered out loud why a lift had not been installed, the same thing happened. I wanted to explore it because the Beatles had recorded a live concert there but once the cameras had whirred, we hit the road. At the Grand Canyon, everybody posed and then asked to leave because it was too hot. In San Francisco, it was too cold. In fact, throughout the tour, the group always wanted to be somewhere else as soon as they had taken their photos.

That grievance, however, was nothing compared to the disgraceful homophobia that we experienced. I will admit that I was eager to visit the gay village of San Francisco to see how liberal it really was. Indeed, it was but it was also an absolute slum, which was depressing. What I did not expect, however, was for my companions to treat the village like a freak show.

As the coach drove through the streets of the village, they asked the driver to slow down so that they could get a better look. Some of the comments from so-called intelligent Singaporeans left me dumbfounded. At first, I wanted to scream at them, then I wanted to cry. By the end, I just felt numb. It remains the worst experience I have ever had with Singaporeans. The children were falling over themselves to get a better look at the 'freaks' while their parents whispered to them that such behaviour was wrong and evil.

I recall one particular boy who said, 'They're holding hands. Ugh, those men are holding hands, mum. It's horrible.' Then all the insane comments came gushing forth.

'It's sick, isn't it? They shouldn't be allowed to do it.'

'Slow down, slow down. That one's wearing make-up.'

'It's not right. It's disgusting. You're not allowed to be like that, okay? It's evil.'

'Why do they do it?'

'Because they're not well. Some can be cured but others can't.'

These comments gave me a knotted feeling in my stomach. I grew up in a very racist, sexist, homophobic environment, as many working-class children do in England, and I wanted to leave that world behind. Of course, I have gay friends in Singapore and I understand the problems they suffer but I had never directly encountered such large-scale Singaporean homophobia before. I am not saying that it does not exist in Britain because it does. However, homosexuality is not considered evil and the country accepts that gays exist. Singaporeans will not and I know that my travelling companions, both young and old, never will. I realised then; it was time to go home.

Chapter Nine

There is nothing like a funeral to really ruin your day. Or to be precise, one tragic funeral that I had to cover as a reporter. A former national footballer had died and I was sent to the family home to interview the relatives. They say it comes with the territory but if I never have to interview grieving relatives again, I will be a happy man. After speaking to the family, I racked my brain in an attempt to conjure the words needed to write an obituary for a man I had never met. As I stood by the roadside, waiting for a taxi, it started to rain and I had no umbrella. What a day this was turning out to be.

I was then blessed with what probably has to go down as the greatest conversation of my life. Finally stepping into a taxi, I was initially startled when the middle-aged Chinese driver turned a full 180 degrees to say hello to me. This has never happened before. At best, the cab driver may nod through his rear-view mirror but usually he just stares straight ahead and says, 'Where you wanna go?' So there is nothing like a set of pearly whites beaming at you to make you want to slip back out of the taxi. Before I had even had the chance to contemplate such a drastic course of action, he spotted my notepad and away he went.

'Ah, you're a writer, is it?'

'Yeah, kind of. I'm a reporter.' I saw his eyes widen in the rear-view mirror and he sat up straight. 'What you write about?'

'Sports, but mainly soccer.'

'Ah, Fandi Ahmad?' he enquired brightly.

Fandi is Singapore's favourite footballing son, a fabulous striker who played for several European clubs. He is now the coach of the Singapore Armed Forces.

'Yeah, I sometimes have to speak to Fandi when his team plays,' I replied but the driver did not seem too interested in this. His fidgety body language suggested he was itching to get something off his chest.

'Listen, I have a story. But no name, eh? Like you say, off the record, okay?'

'Sure, Mr Ong, no problem.' I replied teasingly.

'Hey, how you know my name?' he cried out in despair.

'It's written on the name tag next to your picture, Mr Ong.' He began to look seriously distressed so I stopped teasing him.

'They'll know it's me if you say my name.'

'Who will know it's you?'

'The PAP.'

Now this was getting interesting. The taxi driver was referring, of course, to the People's Action Party, the ruling party of the Singaporean government. Generally speaking, the local men that I have interviewed here are more willing to talk publicly about their penis girth than they are about the negative aspects of the PAP. This guy clearly had something interesting to say. Unfortunately, he was insane.

Staring at me intensely as if he were Travis Bickle, Robert De Niro's character in *Taxi Driver*, he lowered his voice. 'If you get sick, don't go to government hospitals because they'll kill you.'

'What?'

'Never mind what illness you have, if you go government hospital, you will not come out alive.'

'Why?'

'I have a friend who is a doctor. I cannot tell you his name but he told me this so I know it's true. If you are healthy and go to hospital with a little illness, they will cut your organs in a private room and you will die.'

'But why?'

'The government sells the organs to rich people all over Asia.'

'But why?'

'For big money. How you think all big politicians have those large houses and rich cars.'

'Because they're big politicians?'

'No lah, because they make money from selling organs.'

'But Mr Ong...'

'No, no, no! You cannot say my name, okay? Hey! Why you writing? You cannot write, don't write my name down. I only tell you because maybe you can let public know. But you cannot say my name.' This guy was certifiable.

'I'm just writing down the facts for my own benefit. I'm not writing down your name. Believe me, I'll be telling your story to everybody for years. But tell me, how is it kept such a secret from the nation, but you know all about it?' I asked.

'I told you, I've got doctor friend who told me the story. He said that the government doctors who know about it cannot talk or sure get fired. And they earn big money too from the government for this.'

'They must do. What do they do with the organs?'

'They keep them in a freezer until someone buys them.'

I felt a vein near my brain explode with laughter. This was something else. I imagined a secret supermarket in the basement of Singapore General Hospital (SGH) called 'Fair-priced Organs' or 'Lungs R Us' – a place where wealthy big shots silently pushed a shopping trolley along aisles of open freezers that stocked everything from blood pumping hearts to two-for-one kidneys and the cashiers were all prominent politicians doing a spot of moonlighting. My mind wandered all over the place and it was marvellous. A quick change of traffic lights and screeching brakes brought me back to the real world of writing obituaries about dead sportsmen and I sadly realised my unforgettable journey was almost over. Nonetheless, I still had time to stoke the fire one last time.

'Hey! I went to SGH to have my tonsils removed. They gave me a general anaesthetic but when I woke up, all my organs were still there.'

'Ah, you were lucky. They don't really do it to the ang mohs. They prefer to use local parts.'

I was about to say that I was a human being and not a Volkswagen but he was off again.

'Also, easier to use locals, less problems. Easier to cover up. If they use ang mohs, your families and your countries will make checks, what.'

'Well, that's a relief,' I said. 'I want to keep my organs.'

He smiled at me through the rear-view mirror and we pulled over to the kerb.

As I got out, he said, 'Remember always use private hospitals, okay? Are you going to write the story?'

'But of course. It will be on page one on Sunday. It will be above the "Hitler is a trishaw driver" piece and next to the "Elvis was a Singaporean sailor" story. Rest assured, if I am feeling depressed, you will be the first person I call for a story. Take care and try not to dribble when you're driving.'

Of course, I made up the last part. Elvis was actually in the Armed Forces. However, the whole 'hand-over-your-organs' episode always serves as a reminder of how wonderful travel in and around Singapore actually is. The best part is that you get to do it via the wonderful local cabbies.

The island is positively crawling with such cabbies, over 15,000 to be exact, all ready and willing to take your money. They are also a permanent source of amusement for passengers like myself. Perhaps it is rare for them to pick up a Caucasian outside an HDB block in Toa Payoh because they always seem so pleased to see me. Without fail, they will do three things in a specific order. First, they will ask me where I want to go. Then, they will want to know where I am from and my entire life history. Finally, they will tell me about all the ang mohs they have picked up that week, month or year; depending on how talkative they are and how long the journey is. Over the years, I have honed a technique whereby I try to pace my answers because I have a habit of running out of things to say. With the really chatty drivers, I sometimes find myself recalling my favourite childhood memories before I have even left Toa Payoh.

What makes Singaporean cabbies unique is their reliance upon the passenger for navigation. This can be quite bewildering, especially if you have absolutely no idea where the place is, which is often the case for me. Nevertheless, drivers are insistent that you direct them.

'Where you go?' they ask.

'Bukit Batok West, please,' I reply breezily.

'Which way do you wanna go?'

'I'm sorry?'

'Which way you wanna go?'

'Shall we try the quickest?' This answer never seems to satisfy the chap in front and he then dazzles me with incomprehensible alternatives.

'We could go PIE, CTE, then BKE followed by a short stint on the KFC. But there's heavy traffic coming down Bukit Timah, so we could go Chua Chu Kang, then Phua Chu Kang and onto Liang Po Po, which is longer but less traffic. Which way you wanna go?'

'The quickest.'

'Hmm, the quickest. That could be tough unless we go through the CBD, pay extra ERP, turn left past McD and pay extra for the CHILLI. Go right into ABC and learn the rest of the alphabet so we can get to XYZ. Then we'll have to stop because I've run out of sad TLA's (three letter acronyms) that we are so fond of here. Which way you wanna go?'

'The fucking quickest, please!'

'Okay. We'll go down Bukit Batok Road and we should be there in five minutes. So you're from England? Let me tell you all about the ang mohs I've had in my taxi over the last fifteen years.'

And that's the great thing about Singapore – most places are only a few minutes away. For example, from my HDB flat in Toa Payoh, I am a five-minute walk away from shops, various bus stops, the MRT, two major highways, the national police academy, a country club and the Singapore Polo Club. My office is a fifteen-minute bus ride away. In a car, I am fifteen minutes from the beach and only twenty minutes from the causeway that joins Singapore to Malaysia. In short, everywhere is accessible, especially in a taxi, and it leaves me itching to explore.

The irony is that there are some truly wonderful places dotted all over the island and I know that many of my Singaporean friends have not visited half of them. Of course, it is not only Singaporeans who fall into this trap. I have met Americans who have seen the miniature Statue of Liberty overlooking the River Seine in Paris but they have not seen its big sister in New York. At university, I studied with an Egyptian guy who had never been to Luxor to see, among other things, the Valley of the Kings containing Tutankhamen's tomb. He had never seen the point. Yet I remember him getting excited when he told me he had just returned from seeing the historical sites of London.

However, the most ignorant guy I have ever met has to be me. It was only when I came to Singapore that I realised how disgracefully uninformed I am of my own country after speaking to Singaporeans who had seen more of England's treasures as a two-week tourist than I had in twenty years. Having studied and loved history for most of my academic life, I am ashamed to admit that I have never seen Stonehenge, a prehistoric megalithic monument dating from around 3,000 to 1,000 B.C., even though it is only a two-hour drive from my front door. Since moving to Singapore and becoming essentially an English tourist, I have developed a greater appreciation of the heritage of my homeland.

In time, I hope increasing numbers of Singaporeans become more enamoured with their own sights and sounds because there are some real crackers. Let's start with Sentosa Island. It is Singapore's most popular leisure resort, the home of the giant Merlion, which is the symbol of Singaporean tourism, and the place where I got my head smashed in.

Located 500 metres off the southern tip of Singapore, Sentosa was once a military base. Then, in 1972, some bright spark realised the island could bring in a dollar or two so the Sentosa Development Corporation was formed to transform the place into a haven for fun-seeking tourists and locals. Consequently, it has been filled with musical fountains, sound and laser shows, waxwork museums, golf courses and an impressive walk-through aquarium full of sharks and manta rays.

For an island that is just 4 sq. km, there is certainly not a shortage of things to do but my favourite place is undoubtedly Fantasy Island, the water slide park. I have visited similar parks in Spain and Greece but this one is by far the best.

Yet I have a fundamental problem with the logistics of water slides. I have never grasped the basic laws of physics, which dictate that tall, skinny people with legs longer than Cindy Crawford are not built for water slides whereas short, muscular types, i.e. the majority of Singaporeans, most certainly are. Consequently, I have had more kicks in the back of the head than I care to remember.

I am usually cruising down the slide when suddenly I hear the sound of flesh moving quickly through the water above me. More often than not, it is the discernible sound of a stocky teenager, with disproportionately large feet, bearing down upon me. I always try to accelerate but, without the necessary body mass, it is a bit like a paper aeroplane trying to outrun a nuclear missile. Anticipating the swimming pool ahead, a hairy big toe tickles the back of my ear before we fly off the slide as one long body, with the other person's feet clamped around my neck. When we emerge from our underwater embrace, I rub my eyes to find, as usual, that it is a teenage boy. Fate has never once allowed my ear to be tickled by Jamie Yeo or Cameron Diaz.

Fate, however, has conspired to make me stop altogether in the middle of a slide. On one occasion, I watched some teenagers push forcibly against the top of the slide to give themselves a better takeoff so I thought I would try the same thing. With all my feeble strength, I pushed off but I barely moved. It was stunningly pathetic. I stuttered down the slide with all the speed and grace of a dead snail. I realised trouble was brewing when the slide took a sharp vertical turn and my puny body defied all gravity and common sense by actually slowing down. At the same time, I could detect the foreboding sound of a sumo-sized Singaporean coming down the slide like a nuclear submarine. In a state of panic, I performed a kind of jerking motion through the water, which caused two things to happen. First, it produced hysterical laughter from some distant corner of the park. Second, and far more critical, my silly jerking caused me to come to a complete stop. As I lay there, I could hear the water slide world racing champion approaching.

After a prolonged bout of silly jerking, I began my slow descent once again. I could almost feel my pursuer's big toes brushing against the back of my neck. Then, I spotted the end of the slide. Although there were just a few more seconds to go, the guy was almost lying beside me. If I could just turn my body onto my left side, my speeding neighbour could pass on the right and we would both exit the slide together, I thought. Under the panic-stricken circumstances, this has to go down as a wonderfully quick piece of initiative. Waiting until the last second, I flipped my whole body to the left.

'Aah, fuck me!' I cannot apologise for the swearing. I nearly took my head off. As I was about to come off the end of the slide, I had inexplicably turned 90 degrees to the left, just in time to catch my head on the left-hand corner of the slide with such force that it almost knocked me out. Fortunately, a couple of my friends were waiting at the bottom and they later informed me of the semiconscious behaviour that followed. I arose from the water like an intoxicated mermaid, rubbing a lump on the side of my head that was the size of the Merlion. Motioning to say something, I fell over again and swallowed far too much chlorine. Coughing and spluttering, I then informed everybody who cared to listen (and boy, did I have a big audience) that I intended to 'sue this shitty place for every dollar that I can get. I'll have this fucking place closed down in a fortnight. It made me smash my head in. Now, where's First Aid?'

That was not the only time that I have nearly killed myself at a Singaporean attraction. When my sister Jodie and her husband Kirk came to visit a couple of years back, one of the first places I took them to was Bukit Timah Nature Reserve. I was certain it would impress them. How could it not? Bukit Timah is one of only two rainforests in the world within city boundaries, the other being in Rio de Janeiro. At the top of the reserve is Singapore's highest peak, Bukit Timah Hill, which is 164 metres above sea level. In addition, the 164-hectare reserve contains more species of plants than the whole of North America and is home to the black spitting cobra and the Oriental whip snake.

Best of all, cute, but not quite so cuddly, long-tailed macaques also make their home in the reserve. Extremely intelligent, often vegetarian and quite happy to bare their arse to the world, these cheeky chappies are my kind of primate. The only threat they face comes, as ever, from man. Now, if Singaporeans are not throwing up condominiums on prime site land, they are feeding the macaques in Bukit Timah Nature Reserve. Despite signs being posted all the way up the hill reminding visitors why they must not feed the monkeys, they still do. Now you do not have to be an ecologist to realise that feeding the macaques will, to use a technical term, screw up the ecosystem. In time, they will stop finding their own food, thus breaking a link in the food chain. The constant feeding of macaques has already brought them into closer contact with human beings, which is a pressure cooker situation – either the human makes a sudden movement, scaring the monkey and forcing it to hiss through gritted teeth, or the monkey innocently approaches the smallest human in the group, forcing the concerned parent to react.

In these situations, there are two options available. Without alarming the monkeys, you can pick up the pace a little and walk on. Alternatively, you can protect your family of impressionable young children by waving a two-metre-long branch at anything that moves.

On the day that we were at the reserve, the latter option was adopted by a thirty-something Chinese chap who was walking towards us with his wife, the maid and his two young children. Whenever a 30-centimetre-high monkey approached the family, the guy stepped in front of his awe-struck family and, without a thought for his own safety, brought the branch crashing down. After watching the nimble primate easily evade the lumbering manoeuvre of its overweight attacker, it occurred to me that scientists might have made a mistake when calculating the stages of human evolution. How one had supposedly led to the other, I will never know.

It was an embarrassing situation for me. I could see Jodie and Kirk, both vegetarians, looking on with disgust. My sister had only been in the country a week and I was bending over backwards to give her a positive impression of the place. I wanted her to feel the way I did about the country and its people and this apeman was screwing everything up. I could not walk away so I reverted to my subtle, diplomatic disposition.

'Put the fucking stick down,' I found myself shouting.

'What?' the startled monkey-batterer replied.

'Put the stick down. What do you need it for? The monkeys won't hurt you.'

'But they are attacking my children.'

'Don't lie to me. You've got food in your hands. If you feed them, then of course they'll come near you, so put the bloody stick down.'

It was becoming quite tense. As I had confronted him in front of his wife and children, the guy was 'saving face' and refused to put the branch down. With my little sister and her husband watching, I was childishly doing the same. Edging towards the guy, I could see his wide-eyed young children staring at me. What could I do? Have a fight with the moron in the middle of a public park with his two pre-school kids looking on? Of course I could not so I improvised a compromise.

'Are you going to hit the monkeys with that stick?'

'No, I'm just keeping them away.'

'Well, you'd better not.'

With that, we continued walking up the hill. I regretted the use of bad language in the presence of small children but I was quite impressed with my self-restraint and I expected my due praise when we reached the summit. Yet the opposite proved to be the case. Over sandwiches, my girlfriend turned to me and said, 'You should have hit the bastard.' There is just no pleasing some people.

Trying to save a monkey's life was not the highlight of that day. Attempting to save our own necks proved to be the real high point. Looking back now, death seemed like a distinct possibility and I was the foolish one who had almost caused it to happen. I had arrogantly misconstrued the phrase 'big brother living overseas' to mean 'big shot who knows his way around dense rainforest without a guide'. Now you may snigger at this and, of course, I know that Bukit Timah Nature Reserve is hardly Brazil – but forest is forest. Furthermore, when you are covered in scratches and crawling on your hands and knees up a vertical slope amid greenery so thick that you cannot see the sky, I think you are entitled to panic a little. When I told my boss what had happened the next day, she looked at me and said, 'That wasn't very clever. Last year, an experienced trekker went missing in Bukit Timah and was later found dead by a helicopter.' It sent a shiver down my spine. I am not sure if her story is true but I do know that ours was a close call.

The ironic thing was that we were almost on our way home. We had been to the top of the hill and we were making our way down the public footpath when we were confronted by a couple of Indian guys who had just emerged from the forest. Curious, I asked them where they had been and they told us that they had been down to see the quarry. Genuinely intrigued, we followed the tiniest of footpaths into the forest for no more than a hundred metres and found the quarry, which was a magnificent site to behold. My brain started to whirr furiously, which is always a bad sign. On this occasion, it told me to tell the others 'if we found this quarry, a magnificent site to behold, without really trying, imagine what we could find if we explored further'. There was a chorus of 'good idea', 'come on, let's go' and 'Neil, why didn't you smack that guy with the stick?' so I knew that I had the group's committed support for my ill-conceived plan.

Without telling the others, I began to panic after about two hours. We had not really seen any kind of footpath since the quarry, the trees were tall and thorny plants were ripping our bare legs to shreds. None of us were equipped for this kind of trekking and it was almost 5:30 p.m. This meant that not only was the park due to close in half an hour but, far more worryingly, it would start to get dark after 7 p.m. We had no food or drink left, no mosquito repellent and we were positively melting. None of us were wearing hats and I lost count of the number of times that I was scratched on the head by thorns. I was then struck by the terrifying thought – no one knew that we were here. The reserve, sensibly assuming that no one would be foolish enough to leave the footpaths, had no monitoring system that I was aware of. We had not told anyone that we were visiting the nature reserve that day and I had no hand phone then. (Oddly enough, I bought one in Toa Payoh the following day, I cannot think why.) Put simply, we could scream and not be heard, we could jump around and not be seen and I was beginning to wonder if we could die and not be found. At about the same time, everyone in the group suddenly became upbeat and jovial. This artificial mood swing worried me. They, too, shared the same concerns as me.

With six o'clock rapidly approaching, we stopped for a while to think things through. We all agreed later that had we not conceived a viable solution then, we would have seriously started to panic. Something strange then happened. I am not a religious man but I am convinced that a touch of fate made me have one last look around an area that we had already covered with a fine-tooth comb several times. I vividly recall looking over my right shoulder and spotting a huge rock that protruded slightly through the trees. I was certain that we had walked past that rock on the way because I remembered seeing a squashed cola can, which had surprised me seeing as we were so far off the beaten track. Without saying anything to the others, I made my way over to the rock. The mashed-up coke can was by the side of the rock and just beyond it was a footprint made by one of Kirk's trainers. For a brief second, I shared the exhilaration of Howard Carter after he had discovered Tutankhamen's tomb. Then I felt like a man who had not eaten for three hours and I shouted at the others to get a bloody move on.

After reaching the footpath, I decided to use the video camera to record the episode for posterity. When I watch it with others now, I laugh at the craziness of it all. When I watch it by myself, I find myself quite shocked by it. While I recorded, the other three stood still in silence. None of them attempted to make any conversation and they only looked at the camera fleetingly. My girlfriend had a couple of awful gashes on her knee. Kirk was extremely red-faced and, like me, was covered in mud. Poor Jodie was wiping her tear-stained face and trying to regain a regular breathing pattern following a breathing fit she had had a couple of minutes earlier. We certainly learnt from the incident.

Despite the odd horror story, exploring Singapore can be a great laugh. The zoo, with its natural, open concept has to be one of the best in the world, while the first and only time I have stood transfixed was at the Night Safari, which is apparently the world's only night zoo, as a group of giraffes ran together across a field under the cover of darkness with the stars twinkling overhead. It may not be the Serengeti Plain and ultimately the animals are still not free but it is not a bad substitute.

At Sungei Buloh Nature Park, a great wetland reserve that is strangely ignored by many tourists, I encountered the fattest, longest monitor lizard that I have ever seen. It was relaxing by its swamp on a sun lounger, enjoying the midday Sun. For a working-class urchin from Dagenham, it was quite a wildlife experience. In the words of the great Sir David Attenborough, I shat myself. Obviously evicted from Jurassic Park, I was certain the miniature T-Rex was eyeing me up for dinner so I snapped a picture and ran off to change my trousers. Such creatures are rarely spotted down the high streets of suburban London.

Singaporeans complain that there is nothing to do here but, in the next breath, tell me that they have never been to the Night Safari or Sungei Buloh. However, they have been to London Zoo, which is quite simply crap in comparison to the one in Singapore, and Regent's Park. Just like I have never stepped inside St. Paul's Cathedral but I have marvelled at the architecture of Notre Dame in Paris. We are all hypocrites and I intend to make up for lost travels when I eventually return to England.

For a country that is only 42 km long and 23 km wide, the list of things to do, in my opinion at least, is mind-boggling. If Sir Stamford Raffles arrived with his family today, he would be flying down the water slides at Fantasy Island by day and getting sloshed with the other expatriates at Clarke Quay by night. Of course, travel is travel and I would never discourage Singaporeans from taking their families to experience foreign cultures but there is plenty to see here. So jump in a car, preferably your own, and head for the East Coast, Mount Faber, MacRitchie Reservoir or any place for that matter that you have not visited for a few years. I guarantee you will be pleasantly surprised.

Chapter Ten

Sitting on an aircraft almost continuously for 16 hours does several things to the mind and body. First, it turns you into a battery hen with a backside so numb that if you fell out of the window at 30,000 feet and manoeuvred your body to land on it, your backside would save your life. Second, it becomes increasingly evident (Singaporean civil service departments and Singaporean bus companies, please take note here) that there are only so many times you can watch *Mr Bean* before it begins to seriously rankle with your senses.

Worst of all, air travel makes you Game Boy crazy. Or to be more specific, Tetris crazy. This is the game that transforms you not into a swashbuckling detective or a muscle-bound street fighter but into a bricklayer. Your mission, wait for it, is to build countless brick walls as fast as possible. Mark my words, there will always be one snotty-nosed kid, well within earshot, who will play the brick game at full volume while on an aeroplane. Within five minutes, you are left with no alternative but to approach the boy, grab the game out of his hands and whack him over the head with it. Anyone who feels my recommendation is a trifle brusque has obviously never heard the theme tune to Tetris. It is repetitive, childlike and seeps through your brain cells. Weeks later, you can be standing in a queue at the bank and find yourself singing at the top of your voice, 'Do dee do-do do do-dee do-do do do dee do-do do.' This irritating tune eats away at you for the rest of your life.

So imagine how Scott and I felt after 16 hours of all this as we made our way towards Singapore in late 1996. Mr Bean had just fallen off the diving board and lost his trunks again and the kid in front with the runny nose had just started his 485th game of Tetris. We were praying for something stimulating to happen. Having already formulated seventeen different ways to murder a small child with a Game Boy cartridge, I decided to leaf through my guidebook of Singapore.

In just one paragraph, we found our second wind and laughed so much that even snotty-nosed Game Boy paused his wall-building mission to turn around. The book noted that Singapore (i.e., the government) has tried so hard to reshape itself that it has fallen into self-parody. To support this claim, it quoted a Singaporean politician as saying the country had to pursue fun very seriously to stay competitive in the 21st century. What an inspired, unforgettable comment.

Once Scott and I had stopped laughing, we were struck by a worrying concern. What kind of people were we letting ourselves in for? Joking about it was one thing but if foreign observers were complaining that the country was dull and lacking in humour and politicians were responding with such a painfully-serious reply, were we heading towards an island of sombre, humourless Singaporeans?

Sitting open-mouthed and stunned in a cinema a week later, we were terrified that we might have been right. At the risk of being shot down in flames here, the locally produced movie *Army Daze* left us shell-shocked. David had suggested we watch a homegrown movie that would provide us with a slice of local life. It was a comedy that had been adapted from a highly successful stage play about the trials and tribulations of National Service (NS) and had been taking the country by storm. It did not turn the cast and crew into overnight millionaires by any means but at least it did not star Jean Claude van Damme or Sylvester Stallone so it was certainly a step in the right direction. The audience was made up prominently of young male Singaporeans in their twenties, i.e., people like David who had already done their NS and could relate to the story.

About twenty minutes into the movie, our worst fears were being realised. This really was an island of unfunny people. I genuinely believed I was watching the worst comedy since the terrible *Carry On Columbus*. Staring on in disbelief, Scott and I were stunned to find the auditorium roaring with laughter. No matter where we turned, we were faced with young, red-faced Singaporeans with tears streaming down their faces.

Initially, I went for the obvious conclusion that we were from a different culture and, therefore, could not possibly appreciate the localised jokes and the colloquial language. Having been so impressed with the country to that point, I desperately tried to enjoy the movie but the corny gags were relentless and only slightly less predictable than Scott constantly leaning over and shouting 'This film's fucking shit' every other minute. I remember one particular visual 'gag' that still makes me cringe. The limp-wristed, effeminate character, who was obsessed with his appearance, tried on his new army uniform and then walked up and down the corridor as if it were a catwalk. Even the camp *Carry On* movie series of the sixties, which I had watched as a child, had more originality than this. Nevertheless, bladders seemed to be leaking all around me.

Later that evening, I tried to console Scott who was deeply distraught by the whole affair.

'Look Scott, we've only been here a week. We haven't done national service and not all of the film was in English.'

'So? It had subtitles, didn't it?'

'Yeah, but you can't read.'

'Bollocks. I can't believe I had to pay S$7 to watch that shit. Chicken rice is only S$2 and I know which one I'd rather have. And what that fuck were they all laughing at?'

'It's just local humour, isn't it? We couldn't expect them to understand a film that was in a London cockney dialect.'

I was wrong on both counts and I knew it. Humour is universal as that bloody *Mr Bean* has proven over the years. I reminded myself of this just recently when *Army Daze* was repeated on television. Being a sucker for nostalgia, I settled down to watch it with my girlfriend who had never seen it. Guess what? It was still crap. Being more in tune with the local culture, there was only one joke that I had missed the first time. There was a fast-talking, Hokkien-speaking, gambling, streetwise teenager who behaved just like an Ah Beng and whose name happened to be Ah Beng. His character did make me laugh. As for the rest of the movie, well, it seemed dated when it was made and it now seemed prehistoric.

None of this, however, matters any more. I am no longer paranoid about a faceless mass of boring Singaporeans because they do not exist and I am not sure that they ever did. Since coming here, I have encountered more than a handful of funny Singaporeans, some of whom should be receiving psychiatric treatment.

Take crazy Chinese drummers, for example, or one huge Chinese drummer called Ah Heng to be precise. Ah Heng performed the drumming duties for the Tanjong Pagar United Fan Club.

Tanjong Pagar United is one of the professional football teams here and plays in the S-League, the national league. Do not ask me how but I somehow ended up becoming vice chairman of the fan club for a year or so and we managed to win the S-League Fan Club of the Year award in 1998, something that I am quite proud of.

I have always believed that a good testing ground for a community's sense of humour is on the terraces of its local football club. Needless to say, I was delighted to discover that Singaporean football fans also share the piss-taking wit of the terraces. Every time a referee makes a perceived error, one half of the stadium will instantly cry, 'Referee kayu, referee kayu.' After asking around, I learnt that *kayu* means 'wood' in Malay. In this context, then, the referee is 'dead wood' or a 'plank'. I have always loved the word 'plank' ever since I was endlessly called one at school. There are dozens of terms you can use to call someone a moron or an idiot but I love the word 'plank' because it sounds dopey too. Thus, whenever Singaporeans call a referee a plank, they do not hear any complaints from me.

Ah Heng, in particular, was very fond of the term and would scream it over the top of his incessant drumming in the terraces of Tanjong Pagar's football grounds. Now it must be said that he was no Phil Collins but he did have impeccable comic timing. Like football fans the world over, I despise professional footballers when they insult the average supporter's intelligence by performing their dying swan act. It fools no one except that plank with the whistle. We have all witnessed it. The winger breaks free on the left and hares towards the goal just as the chasing full-back accidentally sneezes some ten yards away. Right on cue, the winger goes down as if he has been shot by a cannon and before anyone has even had the chance to call the diver a wanker, the plank arrives to book the defender for the offending sneeze and to nominate the dying man for an Academy Award. To add insult to injury, the winger must now see his performance through and pretend he is really injured so the game is delayed while six fat guys pant and wheeze across the field with a stretcher. Enter Ah Heng, the perturbed percussionist with huge drumsticks. As the 'injured' winger groans theatrically, our drummer strikes up a sombre beat that causes hysterical laughter from the crowd. The first time Ah Heng played this beat, I asked the Chinese auntie next to me what he was playing and she told me it was played at Chinese funerals. Call me insensitive but I thought it was absolutely delightful. By this stage, other drummers had joined in, some of the kids were clapping along and just about everybody was laughing. It was marvellous. The world's worst actor was being carried off to the Chinese funeral march. West Ham fans performed a similar ritual when I was a kid. Whenever an opponent went down, be it genuine or feigned, the West Ham faithful would simultaneously cry 'Nee-naw, nee-naw, nee-naw, nee-naw', mimicking the sound of an ambulance. The Tanjong Pagar fans went a stage further and actually killed off the guy.

However, there is certainly more to life than football and there is certainly more to local humour than S-League football fans. Beginning to feel a little guilty for my savaging of *Army Daze*, I began to look out for other homegrown comedies and so started to watch *Under One Roof*. It is a sit-com based around a stereotypical Singaporean HDB-dwelling family. The wife is a caring but nagging, mahjong-playing housewife who loves to gossip with the neighbours, the daughter is a typical overachieving Singaporean student, one son is a lazy cad obsessed with get-rich-quick schemes and the other is a hypochondriac. These characters make the show watchable for many but, for me, it is the father who is the real scene stealer. His stinging rebukes to his children are razor sharp and he ends every episode with a story of extremely dubious origins.

I mention this character only because I have met Singaporeans who are really like this. My landlord, Uncle Kong, is a fine example. Larger than life, he loves spending time with what he calls his 'big family' and he kindly includes my girlfriend and me in this circle. He started laughing about five minutes after we first met him and I do not think that he has stopped since. No topic of conversation is beyond his amusement. We have discussed our apartment, starting a family, politics, moving back to England, the weather and even the soft drinks sold at a particular chicken restaurant and somehow he has always managed to make a joke out of whatever we have been talking about. The best part is that no one has ever found Uncle Kong's quips funnier than the man himself. We were once discussing the high crime rates in England as compared to Singapore and he immediately put it down to lifts.

'What's it got to do with lifts?' I foolishly asked.

'No good for burglars. Can only carry one thing at a time. Got to take the video, then go down. Come back up, take television, then go back down again. Have a rest, drink *kopi*. Come back up, take VCD player. It takes so long to rob HDB flats. English houses much better. No lifts so can take more much faster. Make more money, lah.'

However, it does not stop at Uncle Kong. At Tanjong Pagar United, we used to have regular fan club meetings and there were plenty of self-deprecating comments. There was a lovely guy called Sunny who, after being congratulated on the birth of his third child, said, 'We're going to call him Shafiq. So now we have Taufiq and Shafiq. Our next baby will be called traffic.' As in most cultures, names are taken quite seriously in the Malay community so for him to make such a joke in a room full of Chinese and Malays may not have been a laughing matter, but it was.

In fact, the younger generations are finding more comical outlets than ever before. In 1999, a small London-based gangster movie called *Lock, Stock and Two Smoking Barrels* sneaked into Singapore with little fanfare. Like most so-called artistic overseas movies, it was put on at the Picturehouse and should have realistically expected a run of around two weeks. If I recall correctly, it was playing to packed houses for at least six weeks and received rave reviews all over the island. I will admit that I had a vested interest because the actors in this film had the same accent as me, a rarity in most movies shown in Singapore. Nonetheless, Singaporeans found it hilarious, proving my theory that what is funny is funny no matter where you are. This was the London equivalent of *Army Daze* in that it was a homegrown movie about a certain London lifestyle. The film's dialogue was even sprinkled with cockney rhyming slang, which is not properly understood outside of London, so I sat in the Picturehouse with a warm glow as the laughter echoed around the auditorium.

If this sounds patronising, then I can only say that the facts do not lie. Singaporeans have traditionally chomped their popcorn while digesting the action fare of Jackie Chan and Sylvester Stallone in films where the humour is usually as subtle as a kick in the testicles. The majority of the *Lock Stock* audience were young Singaporeans. In fact, the audience had a similar demographic make-up to the one watching *Army Daze* back in 1996. Although cinema fans remain the same homogenous bunch in Singapore, their comic tastes are changing. It now takes a little more than just a limp-wristed teenager walking in an effeminate manner to evoke hilarity.

Even to this day, when talking to Western friends, I am still irritated by the negative perceptions of the Singaporean people. The stereotypical notion that the country is populated by passive, dull citizens remains a strong one and all the hip talk of transforming the island into a 'funky town' seems to have had little influence. I cannot think why. The very idea of calling somewhere a funky town smacks of self-parody and therein lies the problem for me. In Singapore, it is not the people who take themselves too seriously but the nation's government. And before anyone bursts a blood vessel, I am not being critical here.

When the PAP took control in 1959, it was hardly the time for fun and games. The fledgling government was left with a hungry population that was living in homes fit for demolition with the kind of sanitation fit for dysentery; not really the time to open a fine bottle of port, chomp on a cigar and crack a few funnies. Only Winston Churchill had that privilege, safe in the knowledge that Nazi troops were only 22 miles from his country's borders.

Naturally, the PAP spent its formative years getting its house in order. Its leaders went about providing modern education and medical facilities for its people and left the one-liners and the corny sound bites to the likes of Kennedy, Reagan, Thatcher and Major (okay, I put the last one in for a laugh). Call me naive but politicians are paid to formulate policy, not to be comedians, bent accountants or war mongers.

The trouble is that politicians are the front-line receptionists to the world. Singaporean politicians are the only Singaporeans that the rest of the planet usually gets to hear and see. My mates back in Dagenham are not going to get to laugh with the piss-taking Tanjong Pagar fans or chuckle at Uncle Kong's old stories but they will read on in disbelief when a high-ranking official makes comments about having to take fun seriously. To an outsider, it sounds like a nation completely devoid of a sense of humour. What other first impression could such a ridiculous comment possibly give?

Almost every day, some faceless bureaucrat gives some bog-standard response to a genuine enquiry in the Forum pages of the *Straits Times*. Whether the subject matter be road tax, crime rates or even the delayed start of a popular radio show, the official rejoinders are always given in an awfully patronising and robotic way. The only thing that surprises me is that the civil servant concerned is happy enough to sign his name to the drivel. Does he have no pride at all? Does his annual bonus mean that much to him? It saddens me because this is the Singapore that is read about all over the world, thanks to the Internet. Westerners cannot be blamed for forming the view that the country is mundane and humourless when these monotonous public replies are endlessly churned out.

The United States gave the world Coca-Cola, Oprah Winfrey and Jim Carrey. England gave football, most of the world's boy bands and *Mr Bean* while Singapore gave civil servants explaining, in a completely staid and restrained way, why lifts in HDB flats may have to be partly subsidised by the taxpayer. Not really funky, is it?

In fact, just the other day I was listening to Capital Gold, a London radio station, on the Internet and the D.J. was bemoaning the state of public services in England's capital, complaining, in particular, about the ambulance service. 'A recent survey,' he said, 'showed that the call-out time for an ambulance is now 18 minutes, yet your local pizza takeaway promises to deliver within three minutes. So I reckon the next time you have a heart attack, order a pizza and ask the delivery boy to drop you off at the hospital on his way back.' Now I thought this was funny. Could you imagine two local D.J.s making a similar wisecrack here? The civil servants would have an absolute field day.

There would be letters to the *Straits Times* from Mr Tan, the PR supervisor for the ambulance call-out timing department, stating something like 'We'd just like to point out that although we thought the D.J.'s comments were quite humorous in a comical sort of way, they were, in fact, quite incorrect. A survey shows that our ambulances arrive at the scene within 17.8 minutes, which would make them the most efficient in the Southeast Asian region and an improvement of some 15 per cent. This statistic is up on last year's figure by 6.8 per cent, which is part of an overall upward trend of 2.5 per cent over the last 4.8 years. By now, I should have confused you with all the statistics and you will have impatiently turned over to the Sports pages to check your 4-D results.' This letter would, of course, be printed next to a letter from Mr Tay, media consultant for the food, health, safety and pizza department, who would seriously rebuke the D.J. for his potentially dangerous misinformation by writing 'It's in the public interest to note that pizza delivery boys are not equipped to carry sick passengers to hospital. Even if there is a basket on the front of the moped, this basket is designed to carry no more than five pizza boxes. Research carried out suggests that the basket could not possibly hold a human being going through the advanced stages of an epileptic fit. According to pizza regulations, any delivery person caught carrying a sick passenger on their moped while on duty risks being transferred to a burger outlet.' Such letters appear almost every day and the rest of Singapore, including many of the politicians that these letter writers supposedly represent, is left with no choice but to cringe in embarrassment.

However, I am determined to show that the average man, woman or child on the street is not like that. Let's face it, civil servants are boring the world over, otherwise they would not be civil servants, would they? So we can throw them out of the equation and preferably into a bottomless pit. Singaporeans from all walks of life generally have a great sense of humour and they can laugh at others and, more importantly, at themselves. Being able to look in the mirror and laugh at yourself (I do every day – if you have seen me, you will understand why) is the only true test. Of course, there will always be a small group of people who take themselves a little too seriously and have the potential to screw everything up both in England and Singapore. And it is our duty to slap them into place.

Let me give you a very relevant example. When I was young, we used to have a caravan on a site in Clacton-on-Sea, a seaside town in Essex. It was an enclosed site that had a narrow gravel road snaking through and around it. Built only to serve caravan owners, the road was not wide enough to take two cars going in opposite directions so the site owner made it a one-way system. This was most convenient if your caravan happened to be near the entrance; ours was not so we had to take a tour of the site every time we wanted to get to it. Well, we would have done if my mother had wielded such admirable patience. Instead she decided to short fuse the circuit by going the wrong way round the one-way system. Considering the site was not exactly crawling with traffic, it was only a minor misdemeanour. She did not drive fast and, besides, driving into a ditch periodically to avoid an oncoming car was part of the holiday fun.

The only real obstacle we had to clear was a man who had his caravan parked at the junction between the right and wrong way.

A profoundly tedious man, he sat on a deckchair by the edge of the road and leapt into action whenever he detected a car (usually ours) driving in the wrong direction. Hands waving, he would run forward crying, 'Sorry, you'll have to turn back. It's a one-way road. Sorry, you'll have to turn back.' Being a lanky chap with long arms, he resembled a windmill. Initially, my mother would pacify him with the 'sorry, we're new here' routine and he would send us on our way with a warning.

After three years, my mother's defence began to wear a bit thin. On one memorable sunny afternoon, my mother took her regular shortcut. From nowhere came the boring, windmill man. With his hands gesticulating all over the place, he shouted, 'One way! One way! This is a one-way road.' Without missing a beat, my mother retorted, 'Well, that's okay then. We're only going one fucking way.' The windmill, who I am sure was a civil servant, never bothered us again. Sitting in his beloved deckchair, he would start to get up, spot my mother and force himself to smile and wave, making the conscious decision never to let his children play with me or my sister.

Dull people are universal and it is our duty to keep them in place. I read a letter in the *Straits Times* recently that was responding to an earlier piece about Singapore's income divide and how statistics can cloud the issue. The first letter stated, quite rightly, that a typical household's income could be calculated in many ways so we should treat figures with caution. The reply to this letter was something else. I think the guy was saying that the median income was a better yardstick for household income than the mean but I am not really sure. Take a dose of caffeine and read on.

The writer said things like 'The sample of households excluded those with no earned income and the typical household size was

3.6 persons. Thus, a household in the sample could have more than one income earner.' He went on in a similar vein for another seven riveting paragraphs before concluding 'The median is clearly a better gauge of average income. It mitigates any perception of income divide created by the mean.' As conclusions go, they do not come any punchier than that, do they? This mathematician could have teamed up with the windmill to form a double act. They could have sat in matching deckchairs, discussed Pythagoras and shouted 'one way' at moving vehicles all day.

That, however, is only if we let them. These dreary souls are still in the minority and we should be constantly on the lookout to keep it that way. If you are at work or at a party and someone makes a soporific comment involving statistics, money, property or the civil service, shoot the person. Plead to the judge that you did it on compassionate grounds to prevent the spread of what is commonly known as boringfuckeritis and the judge will throw the case out. Alternatively, send the afflicted to the terraces of Tanjong Pagar United for a season or refer him to Uncle Kong for a weekly consultation. Episodes of *Friends* and *Under One Roof* can also be administered. It is imperative that the symptoms are detected at the earliest possible stage to prevent them from spreading. In rare cases where the sense of humour has almost withered away, a literary injection of Spike Milligan, the legendary former goon, must be given immediately.

Should this extreme measure fail, then the victim is left with no other option than to pay up his life insurance and join the civil service. At least, the sick man will be in the company of other victims and he will get to spend the rest of his life pursuing this business of fun very seriously. Fortunately, most Singaporeans that I know have been spared this horrific disease but, for goodness sake, do not pursue every business you undertake too seriously. Look in the mirror each day, laugh at yourself and issue a dry slap to every boring person you encounter. Together, we can prevent this tragic social illness from spreading.

Chapter Eleven

I have just got off the telephone from my mother and the call reminded me that, like most English mothers, she has two voices that are interchangeable. Mothers have an additional gene that can distort their vocal cords to produce their normal voice and a second, 'telephone' voice. The latter is triggered by an involuntary muscle spasm, which is the brain's defensive reaction to the sound of a ringing telephone bouncing off its neighbouring eardrums. Only mothers suffer from the telephone voice syndrome.

My own mother has had this syndrome for years. If it was a typical day, she would be screaming at us in her normal voice for not performing an exceedingly trivial task. 'If you don't put the bloody towels back on the rack properly, you're both gonna get it.'

'Sorry mum,' we would murmur in self-defence, hoping that our feeble apologies would pacify her. They did not.

'And Neil, I don't know why you bothered showering in the bath. You might as well have just stood on the carpet outside and showered yourself on it. Why do you keep spending so much time in the bathroom anyway? It's not normal behaviour.'

'I was just washing my hair, mum.'

'Washing your hair? You haven't got any hair and what you

did have is now sitting in the plughole. Is there any chance of you actually cleaning the bath when you're finished? I can't believe what a pair of lazy bastards I've brought up. Jodie, do you think you could tidy your bedroom? No, I suppose I'll have to do it as usual.'

That was the other thing about my mother, she always answered her own questions. So essentially, she was arguing with herself. Then the telephone would start ringing, which meant a temporary reprieve.

'There's the bloody phone now,' my mother would complain. 'Like I don't have enough to do already. I don't know why I'm even answering it. It's probably for you.'

Then as she lifted the receiver, the syndrome mysteriously kicked in and she went from being our mother to sounding like the Queen Mother.

'Hellooo, this is 2689. Can I help you...? Sylvie, how are you? Are you still working at the supermarket? Oh, that's wonderful because you wanted to work that shift, didn't you? I am pleased for you.'

She would then continue talking in this affected, BBC-styled voice that made her sound like the actress Judi Dench. The beauty of the syndrome for us was that she could not possibly use both voices at once so we would take our cue to have a fight on the living room floor. Having a smaller sister meant there would be the usual tears, headlocks and bruised dead legs but I would hang in there. By the time we were belly flopping off the top of the settee onto each other, we knew that the Queen Mother would need to make a royal pardon.

'Do excuse me, Sylvie. Could you please hold on for just a second? I have to take care of something.' My mother would then regally place the receiver against her chest, perform the royal wave and beckon her two scrapping children to pause momentarily.

'If you two don't stop right now, you're both gonna get it. Sit down and shut up or you'll be getting no fucking dinner… So sorry about that, Sylvie. Now, you were saying about your husband's vasectomy.'

When I grew taller, making it harder, but not impossible, for my mother to crack me across the head, I asked her why she put on a 'posh' voice whenever she answered the telephone.

She replied, 'You have to play the game. You never know who is going to be on the other end and you don't want to give the wrong impression, do you?'

Now I am not sure if my mother is in contact with the Singaporean prime minister but I feel her presence here, too. The way Singaporeans converse has become a national obsession over the last year or so. It began with Senior Minister Lee Kuan Yew who hinted that Singaporeans should polish their English. Before you could say government policy, Prime Minister Goh Chok Tong had introduced the 'Speak Good English' campaign. In other words, Singaporeans had to 'play the game' and adopt my mother's telephone voice to ensure that friends, colleagues and business acquaintances could understand them correctly, thus creating a favourable impression.

Being a former speech and drama teacher, my initial knee-jerk reaction was that the government had implemented a rational, logical policy to help improve business communications flow between East and West. I have met many expatriates working here who have experienced difficulty understanding locals on a day-to-day basis and vice versa. Quite surprising, perhaps, when you consider that the official working language of Singapore is English.

Every Singaporean student must learn English at school, irrespective of ethnic or cultural background.

Where then is the problem? Well, take the movie *Army Daze* for instance. Having been in the country for only a week, Scott and I could not understand some of the dialogue that was allegedly in English. This was mainly because it was not in English but rather Singlish, the local dialect of Singaporean English (some would say it is even a separate language) that is the result of the ethnic melting pot that exists on the island.

With Singlish, you often end up with the word 'can' at the end of sentences, rather than at the beginning, much like *ke yi* in Mandarin or *boleh* in Malay. Exclamations like *lah, aiyoh, meh* and *alamak* often find their way into Singlish, too. However, it is the vocabulary of localised English that I would like to emphasise because this is the most important aspect of Singlish.

In my last job, I enjoyed antagonising my Canadian friends by reminding them that, as a native-speaking Englishman, I had never encountered an English dialect that I could not understand. This fact is true but hardly a big deal, considering I cannot speak any other language. Canadians like my good friend Shawn, on the other hand, struggle with any accent that is not North American. When he saw the movie *Trainspotting*, he confessed that he needed the subtitles to understand the dialogue, as the cast spoke with strong Scottish accents.

As the British Isles is blessed with having so many different accents and dialects scattered over such a small area, I was confident, therefore, that Scott and I would have no problems coming to grips with the local tongue. English is English after all. However, some of what Singaporeans speak most certainly is not English and this is where we encountered some difficulty. What was even more worrying was that as I began to teach in Singaporean schools, it became apparent that students did not even realise that many of the words they spoke were not English. Even if they spoke slowly and adopted my mother's resonant telephone voice, words like *kiasu, kaypoh,* meaning 'nosy', and *gong-gong,* meaning 'silly' or 'stupid', were still being uttered. After discovering what these words meant, I went back to my classes and told disbelieving pupils that these words were not part of the English language. I recall one particular teenage boy who refused to accept that kiasu and kaypoh were not English words. He explained, quite rationally I thought, that these words were spoken by Singaporeans of all races and they could be heard and read in the national media. Although I agreed with him, I added that they were unique to the Singaporean vocabulary and would not be understood in other parts of Asia, let alone in places like England and the United States.

However, Scott and I were eager to fit in. Although we could understand most of a Singlish conversation, we still tried to learn some of its non-English words. The result was a most bizarre linguistic concoction. It must be explained that coming from strong working-class backgrounds, Scott and I had seemingly unshakeable Yorkshire and cockney accents, respectively. Now I hope you will appreciate that it is not easy to completely change the way you speak. But we had no choice. To get by in the coffee shops and mini-marts in Toa Payoh, a smattering of Singlish had to come into play for both of us.

At this point, you may wonder why we did not just learn Malay or Mandarin. I did learn conversational Malay to communicate with Saudita, my crazy old Indian landlady, but I never did discover the Malay for 'Can you please put some bloody clothes on?'

As for Mandarin, well, let's just say that some Singaporeans can be a wee bit obsessive about it. I think it is the four different tones of the language that does it. When I first arrived in Singapore, I was naturally wide-eyed and keen and would try to pick up a few words in Mandarin every day and then test them out on the secretaries or the Chinese teachers at work. For some reason, they would jump all over me. Apart from being laughed at, which I did not mind, there would always be the cry of 'Wrong tone! Wrong tone! It's in the wrong tone, ha ha. You're saying x not y.' Fair enough if this response had been now and then but it was relentless and rarely constructive. My attempts to learn Mandarin were gleefully ripped to shreds so I thought, 'Sod it, life's too short.'

Once we had decided to boycott the idea of actually learning a whole new language because we are lazy buggers, Scott and I decided to have a stab at Singlish. My God, did we sound awful. It was especially tough for Scott. In Britain, the demographic and sociological make-up is such that the further north you travel, the further away you go from Standard English and the more unintelligible the local tongue becomes. This linguistic phenomenon peaks at the top of the island in Scotland's John O'Groats, where its residents are only understood by relatives, neighbours and the local sheep population. Being from Leeds, I suppose Scott was somewhere in the middle of all this. He once told me that people from other parts of Yorkshire could not understand him, so try to picture how he must have sounded to a typical Singaporean once he had added a Singlish slant to his strong northern brogue. He would approach some poor auntie in a fast-food outlet and ask, 'Ellow, ken ye ge' meh eh tool piss cliss-beh chickin se', wi chips 'n eh cork, ken lah?' Although I sympathised with the clueless auntie, it was a priceless cultural encounter. It was made even funnier by Scott's attempt to localise his accent by throwing in 'can lah' at the end, almost as an afterthought. But if there was ever a monumental coming together of two great cultures, it had to be the first time Scott combined English and Singlish to pass a derogatory comment about someone pushing past him on the MRT. 'What a kiasu cunt,' he said simply.

However, as time passed, language became quite a sensitive issue for Scott. Despite his commendable efforts to take the rough edges off his Yorkshire accent, he was struggling to be understood.

'This is Singapore, not Leeds. You can't expect them to understand you when you go onto building sites or meet other architects,' I said to him.

'I know that but I'm bloody proud of the way I talk. I'm not ashamed of it.'

I had to agree with him. When we were at university, our accents, though completely different, were one of the things that bonded us. We were social lepers – no more than a tiny minority of working-class students who raised eyebrows every time we opened our mouths. Many in this situation reached a compromise and went for a more acceptable accent to fit in. Let's face it, we have all met Singaporeans who have studied in the United States and miraculously developed impressive American accents within a year or two. Be deeply suspicious of these people. Having worked with speech therapists, I have been told that it takes considerable effort to completely reshape your speaking voice so I often wonder what the motives of these pseudo-American Singaporeans really are.

As far as Scott and I were concerned, we were not going to change our voices for anybody at university. Instead we went to the opposite extreme and perfected the most common-as-muck style accents you could possibly imagine. I sounded like Michael Caine on speed and Scott spoke as if he had spent his entire life as a farmhand in rural Yorkshire. It was beautiful. We deliberately went out of the way to demonstrate that what we had to say was far more important than how we said it. And it worked.

I tried to explain to Scott that we could get away with the whole accent thing in England because our audience had been exposed to various dialects. The majority of Singaporeans, however, have only really been exposed to two types of English – Asian English and Hollywood English – and we spoke neither. We had no choice but to do the one thing that we would have ripped our tongues out before doing in England: compromise. Eventually, we got by but Scott was never allowed to order a chicken meal again.

Our predicament was a useful case study that I used to share with my secondary students. By all means speak Singlish at home and with friends, I would tell them, just as I would speak cockney in London, but, at the same time, they needed to have both the capability and the awareness to switch to Standard English when appropriate. Apply different codes of communication to different audiences, I said.

The trouble was that I did not believe in what I was saying. I have to confess that in the first six months or so my Western prejudices came to the fore. I thought Singlish was a joke – a complete mishmash of a dialect that was awful on the tongue and ugly on the ear. The sooner it was banished from Singapore completely, I thought, the better for all those with eardrums. I believed that I was on a mission to correct the horrendous speech faults of every student I came across. Working with youngsters who said 'one, two, tree' and believed that words like *siaow*, meaning 'crazy', were actually English, I failed to understand how they were going to be taken seriously in a so-called globalised economy.

Eventually though, I changed my mind for various reasons.

The most obvious being that I actually started to learn Singlish, thus eradicating my ignorance. I had noticed that good friends like David and Victor tried to standardise their English around me, assuming that I would understand them more easily. The only way around this artificial, uncomfortable situation was for me to speak Singlish back to them as and when I could.

Then, I came across one or two middle-class, well-to-do Caucasians who spoke impeccable English and revelled in mocking Singlish at every opportunity when Singaporeans were not around. They would say things like 'Shall we go to the cinema, lah?' or 'May I have a cup of coffee, lah?', placing heavy emphasis on the 'lah' and sometimes even punctuating the word in the air, using their fingers to mime quote marks. For me, the annoying punctuating alone ranks right up there with incest and warrants a lethal injection.

At first, I would smile politely but it soon became apparent that it just was not funny. Largely because I knew that these same arrogant arseholes would have been ridiculing cockney or some other localised accent had they been in England. These wealthy wankers were the same people I had rebelled against at university and I was buggered if I was now going to sit with them in Orchard Road and take the piss out of the average Singaporean on the street.

Therefore, I did a complete 360 degree turn and began to champion the use of Singlish in everyday situations. I still reiterated the importance of speaking Standard English to my students and banned the use of Singlish in class but the trick is knowing when to switch from one to the other. Even my old boss, Juliet McCully, who set up the Speech Therapy Unit at Singapore General Hospital and one of the first speech and drama centres in Singapore, spoke positively of Singlish, explaining that communication was, in essence, all about transmitting your message successfully. How you did it depended entirely on your audience. Even now when I visit England, I revert back to cockney when I am speaking to friends, partly because it is my natural accent and mainly because I do not want them to assume that Singapore has transformed me into a rollneck wearing, Volvo-driving, suburban-living twat. When I go shopping or eat at a coffee shop, I throw in a bit of Singlish and when I am at work, I spontaneously use this bizarre Singlish/English concoction that is neither one thing nor the other.

Then along came the government's Speak Good English campaign, which has the potential to wreck everything. If it was called the 'Speak Good English When Necessary' campaign, you would not hear a peep out of me but it is not. Being a former teacher, I initially thought that the campaign could not do any harm. Although I admire Singlish, I still come across countless Singaporeans who cannot speak anything else. Thus, I thought the campaign could be a success if it could raise the awareness of Standard English in conjunction with its many varieties. The campaign, however, used a sledgehammer to swat the tiniest of flies.

Before you could say 'kiasu reaction', Singaporeans across the nation were encouraged to speak Standard English as often as possible. Television and radio presenters were asked not to slip into their local tongue. Local English-speaking actors were redubbed to remove any traces of a Singlish accent, which served only to make them sound bloody awful. Finally, and most ridiculously, Phua Chu Kang was sent for English lessons – a course of action that raised, for me at least, memories of taking fun seriously.

Phua Chu Kang is the name of the lead character in one of the local comedies. A money-grabbing building contractor, he is an over-aged Ah Beng who plays the fool and speaks nothing but

Singlish. He often reflects the attitudes of the man in the street, albeit in a farcical way. The powers that be were concerned that, among other things, impressionable (and supposedly stupid) Singaporeans would be duped into thinking that his awful English would be interpreted as the standard version and adopted around the island. Thus, it was advised that the character be sent for English lessons in the show. Although the show remained quite funny, I found the storyline depressing. It missed the point of Phua Chu Kang's humour. To understand many of the show's jokes, you must know the correct pronunciation for unusual words. For instance, Phua Chu Kang always gets a laugh when he says 'façade' because he pronounces it 'fer-car-day'. Now if Singaporeans did not know how to say this word correctly, how on earth would they find it funny?

The infuriating thing is that the English campaign came about at a time when Singaporeans, I feel, were beginning to take a real pride in their version of English. Like Changi Airport or the Merlion, Singlish is something that is quintessentially Singaporean. It is a dialect that everybody speaks and understands and is something that could provide the cornerstone for a unifying cultural identity. For the first time, movies like *Money No Enough* and *12 Storeys* were not only being shown on the big screen but, more importantly, their characters spoke the language of the Singaporean on the street. Their mix of Hokkien and Singlish made the jokes and situations seem funnier to Singaporeans because they were more identifiable and realistic. Other local movies like *Liang Po Po* soon followed. Although they were not as successful as *Money No Enough*, it became evident that Singlish and the average man on the street was becoming hip. Forget Tom Cruise, actors like Jack Neo and Gurmit Singh were speaking the language of their audience. It was cool to be like Phua Chu Kang. The cynical side of me suggests this trend shift was one of the factors that prompted the government to act. Speaking like Jim Carrey was one thing but speaking like Liang Po Po, well, that was a different mouthful of words altogether.

The question is: is Singapore trying to build a cultural identity or not? With so many races and cultures all living under one roof, it is extremely difficult to draw out unifying features but Singlish is certainly one of them. It is the language of Singapore and something to be proud of, just like cockney is for Londoners. As long as Singaporeans are aware that they must switch into Standard English when conversing with foreigners, as Scott and I had to, then frankly I do not see what the problem is.

Chapter Twelve

One Saturday morning, Scott and I decided to play football. We purchased one of those cheap, plastic balls at the mini-mart and set off to find a football pitch. After an hour, we had found only two pitches and they were both private school pitches. Out of sheer desperation, I did something that I am still embarrassed by to this day. I went into the school looking for a teacher, which was quite difficult as it was a Saturday, to ask if we could use one of the pitches. As bold as could be, I strolled into the gymnasium and, I am blushing now just thinking about it, approached the PE teacher who was working with a group of teenage students.

In the middle of their gymnastics lesson, I said, 'Hi there. I'm sorry to bother you but I work here as an English teacher and my colleague and I were wondering if we could use your football pitch for a while, just to get some practice, you know.'

'Er, yes, I suppose so,' the stunned man replied. And as calm as you like, I went back out to tell my 'colleague' the good news.

Since becoming familiar with the local education scene, I realise how bizarre I must have looked that day. In a small neighbourhood school in Toa Payoh on a quiet Saturday afternoon, a 1.92 m Caucasian wearing Bermuda shorts and holding a plastic ball that only nursery kids play with walked into the middle of a Co-Curricula Activity (CCA) and asked if he could have a kick about on their pitch. If you had been that young teacher, what would you have said? Whenever I pass that school now on the bus, I always recount the story to whoever I am with and they cannot believe what a prat I was.

Playing football that day brought it home to both Scott and me that you can take the man out of England but you cannot take England out of the man. We both grew up in an environment that had a dominant football culture and we are both extremely passionate about sports in general. Thus, we were delighted to discover that Singapore has a professional football league known as the S-League, which meant that we would be able to attend football matches here. Like most things in Singapore, our local team, Balestier Central, was virtually on our doorstep. The team's first match was away to Geylang United over in Bedok and we decided, quite impulsively, to go. Just as we used to do in England, we found out where the stadium was, plotted our route and decided where we would eat before the game. We subconsciously re-enacted all our prematch rituals. Strangely, I had no expectations whatsoever and I ended up being impressed despite the match being an anticlimactic 0-0 draw.

Aside from the football, we were both struck by the same negative observation. There were non-Singaporean football shirts everywhere. To be more specific, there were Manchester United and Liverpool shirts everywhere and hardly anyone was wearing Geylang or Balestier shirts. On entering the stadium, Scott and I had been given Geylang United polo shirts as free door gifts. We went straight to the toilet to put them on even though we were there to watch Balestier. Yet as we proudly stepped onto the terraces in our new Singaporean football shirts, we were greeted by the sight of more United jerseys than we had seen in Manchester's city centre.

To our astonishment, the Geylang-Balestier match was not a fluke gathering of English football fans. Take a walk down Orchard Road on any given day and look out for the English Premiership jerseys. They are everywhere, both on people's backs and in shop windows. Many shops even stock West Ham United shirts, which amazes me, although I have noticed that they are usually quite dusty and covered in mothballs.

Being an Englishman, I have to put my hands up and admit that my knowledge of the English Premiership certainly did me no harm when I began to teach in Singaporean secondary schools. In the beginning, it was comforting to know that I had something in common with many of the students. Furthermore, it was most convenient, initially at least, for both Scott and me to be able to pick up a newspaper or switch on the television and find out how Leeds and West Ham had performed the day before.

After a while, the apathy towards local soccer began to irritate us a little. We watched Balestier on a semi-regular basis and took quite an interest in the S-League. We bought a couple of S-League shirts and began to look forward to our Saturday night football match ritual. However, we were in the minority. We asked many of our Singaporean friends to join us but no one was interested. Furthermore, many of my students could name the girlfriends or wives of the Manchester United players as well as recall the date of Ryan Giggs's birthday but they could not name more than half a dozen S-League players. The ones that they could name were always the usual suspects such as Fandi Ahmad, V. Sundramoorthy and Nazri Nasir; in other words, seasoned national players who had been around for years.

The reasons for such a lack of interest in local football and sports in general are painfully obvious. Singaporeans want winners. For many years, football gave them just that courtesy of the Malaysia Cup (formerly the Malaya Cup). Started in 1921, it was a Malaya tournament involving Singaporean and Malaysian football teams. Just like the old home internationals between England and Scotland, there is nothing like a contest between two rival neighbours to set the blood racing. The best part was that Singapore won the Cup several times and tens of thousands of Singaporeans turned out on both sides of the Causeway to see it happen. At the end of 1994, however, both the Malaysian and the Singaporean soccer bodies decided that they should go their separate ways and focus on building their own leagues.

The S-League was born in 1996 and Singaporean teams started playing each other instead. With the island being so small, the talent pool is obviously limited and the fan base of each club is even smaller. Consequently, the playing standards and the numbers on the terraces have dipped tremendously from those glorious Malaysia Cup days. There is also nothing like the added incentive of national pride to make you play and cheer that little bit harder, but that too died, to a certain extent, in 1994.

Moreover, no self-respecting kiasu parent is going to allow his or her child to pursue football, or any other sport for that matter, as a long-term career when the chances of success are very slim. Sports can be played at school, and possibly at the weekends when all the homework is finished, but that is about it. I mean, how could you let your son pursue his dream of being the next Fandi Ahmad and earn up to S$5,000 a month when he could probably earn that in a week working for a dot.com company? I have to say that when I was involved with the Tanjong Pagar United Fan Club,

I noticed that the Malays tended to have a slightly different perspective. Many were more philosophical in the sense that if football was an opportunity for an improved standard of living, then so be it. After all, Fandi Ahmad had a tough, kampung upbringing and now he is a millionaire and a role model for the Malay community and Singapore in general. In contrast, Chinese Singaporeans tend to play the odds carefully. They believe that a child who hits the textbooks more often than he hits the back of a net has a greater chance of financial success.

Unfortunately, such an attitude can only have one result. In February 2001, the Singaporean national team competed in some pre-World Cup qualifying matches at the National Stadium. Not a single player in the starting XI was Chinese. They were either Malay or Indian. Knowing that this country has over four million people from which to choose its sportsmen and women, 77 per cent of whom are Chinese, the implications are obvious. Unless rare exceptions like discus thrower James Wong or the swimmer Joscelin Yeo come along on a regular basis, sporting glory will remain the stranglehold of countries that regard sports as more than just something to watch on television or, worse yet, to place a bet on.

Just listen to this. I was sitting at my desk eagerly waiting for the first English FA Cup final of the new millennium to start. I had a vested interest. Turning to a colleague, I said, 'I hope Chelsea wins today.'

'But you're not a Chelsea fan, are you?' she asked curiously.

'Oh, it's not for me. It's for my brother.'

Then she said something that I thought was outrageously funny. 'Why? Did he "take" Chelsea to win?'

'"Take" Chelsea to win? He's only nine years old. He doesn't "take" teams. He supports them. How many nine-year-olds do you know that hang out in betting shops?'

But wait, there is more. During the Euro 2000 tournament, another colleague was upset because her beloved Italy had lost in the final. I consoled her by saying, 'At least your team made it to the final, my team didn't get past the qualifiers.'

A friend walking past at the time heard this and enquired, 'Who was your team then?'

'England, who else?' I replied, somewhat perplexed.

'Yeah well, I'm Singaporean but I don't always "take" Singapore. Sometimes I take Thailand.'

We were on different wavelengths. I was talking about supporting a team; he was talking about 'backing' a team. Do not get me wrong. When Scott and I were studying in Manchester, we would pop over to Ladbrokes every Saturday morning for a little flutter on the Premiership. We were serious punters and sometimes we would go all the way and bet £1 but never against our own team.

However, this is where gambling takes on a whole new meaning. My very first assignment as a sports reporter here was to interview an English football player who had been called up by the Corrupt Practices Investigation Bureau (CPIB) for questioning. He played in defence for a team that was competing in the S-League and his team had been throwing in some crazy goals at the time. He was found not guilty of match fixing but the impression I get from some players is that match fixing, so prevalent in this part of the world, still goes on in the S-League. Simply because gambling is everywhere.

When Singapore Pools legalised football betting in 1999, S-League attendances mushroomed overnight and matches took on a certain edge for some people. When I was helping out with the fan club for Tanjong Pagar United, I vividly recall one Chinese chap sitting a few seats away who was positively beside himself with anxiety. He was off his seat every few seconds, screaming the most awful abuse at the referee. Unless he usually sat in another part of the stadium, which I seriously doubt, I suspect that it was the first time that he had been to the ground; just a week after the betting system had been introduced. Call me a cynic but you can spot a genuine fan from a fake one just by reading a person's body language and this guy was definitely a phoney.

Of course, local sports gambling must be put into perspective. I know for a fact that the majority of fans are not there for financial reasons. Nor are they there to beat the living daylights out of their opponents' supporters. I have yet to find a grunting ape with tattooed forearms and cropped hair sitting on an S-League terrace and singing 'You're gonna get your fucking 'ead kicked in.' I have, however, encountered quite a few of these gentlemen at West Ham matches in England. I have even had the pleasure of being punched on the jaw by one of them. This happened at a reserve match when a drunken cripple on crutches (I am not making this up) mistook me for a Millwall supporter. In contrast, I have witnessed nothing serious in the stands of the S-League. Although there was one particularly heated conversation that almost become serious. A lovely auntie and a dedicated Tanjong Pagar fan once gave Scott two fingers of a Kit-Kat while I only got one. This left me quite antagonistic but I retained my composure and let the woman off with a stern warning.

Chocolate bars aside, I enjoy watching S-league matches as and when I can. Each club now has a small base of dedicated supporters who bring some atmosphere to the games and there is little risk of me being clumped by a drunk old man. I just feel that the local football scene and Singaporean sports in general could be much bigger and more lucrative if they were not hindered by kiasuism and their lack of social status.

Tragically, this mindset applies to the arts too. Singaporeans are more than happy to drag themselves to the cinema every week to marvel at Western talents like Tom Hanks – it is the national pastime. However, if a Singaporean child told his parents that he wanted to be a singer or an actor, I think we both know what the response would be. After all, where is the financial security in that? Prancing around on stage every night is not going to pay for the maid, let alone the condominium to put her in.

Of course, the situation is not helped by the likes of James Lye. For those who are not familiar with his work, Lye was a handsome, hardworking Singaporean actor. In fact, I will have to be honest and say that he is extremely good-looking as my other half constantly reminded me every time he stepped into frame. In Singaporean terms, he was at the peak of his professional powers. He came across as a pleasant guy and he delivered the goods on both English and Chinese shows. He had even crossed over to Hong Kong-financed movies, which were distributed across the region. He was, undoubtedly, a decent role model for budding local actors.

What did he go and do? He quit working in television to become a product manager with one of the largest banks in the region. Far be it from me to question his motives as I am sure the guy had valid reasons for making such a radical career shift. When I heard the news, however, two things struck me. First, and perhaps predictably, the media and the general public by and large saw the move as a positive one as he faced greater financial prospects in the long term, better chances of promotion and all that other materialistic bullshit. The more worrying concern for me, and I know I am being idealistic here but I do not care, was what kind of message was being sent out regarding the local arts industry? Something like 'For heaven's sake, do not consider a career in the arts, the exposure is good but the pay is terrible' or 'Give up your dreams, put on your best smile and sell your bank's lucrative interest rates to wealthy investors.' Call me naive but I did not think that was what the arts was supposed to be about.

Two of my big screen heroes, Robert De Niro and Al Pacino, lived hand to mouth in their early acting days but they did not quit. Somehow, I could not imagine De Niro going up to Martin Scorsese and saying, 'Yeah, I know *Taxi Driver* will be great exposure but I'm in a bit of a pickle. You see, First National Bank has offered me this great desk job and the hours are fixed. There's even a subsidised canteen and, wait for this, I get a travel allowance to boot. I've got my long-term security to think about, you know.' It just would not happen, would it? And before the obvious retort comes in, these guys were not always earning millions of dollars per film but they still took the gamble.

Like I say, only James Lye will know why he really quit the acting profession. It was the public reaction that was so depressing. My cynical friends said that he was probably commanding the sort of high salary in his new job that would tempt the devil himself. Please do not tell me that it just comes down to the filthy lucre again. It is bad enough that we now have to watch uncomfortable Singaporean actors try to deliver their lines in Anglicised accents. Do we want to eradicate them completely by encouraging them to take up secure positions in the corporate world? There is enough American rubbish on television as it is and I, for one, would like to see this junk continue to be diluted a little with more local productions. Singapore is not the biggest of islands and if it discourages the very few talented young performers that it has from pursuing a career in the arts, then this country will never be able to take the business of fun very seriously.

The infuriating irony for me is that I know that talent is out there. I am no scout but I can certainly tell a good actor from a bad one. When I worked as a speech and drama teacher, I was convinced that there were a couple of rough diamonds that had the potential to be polished. After lessons, I discreetly informed these students that I believed they had potential in the dramatic arts. In return, they shot me looks that suggested I had just told them that each of them had the makings of a fine pimp.

Undeterred, I pursued the issue and offered to pass them telephone numbers of some television casting agents but to no avail. They told me that they intended to be engineers or lawyers because that was what they and their parents supposedly wanted. Both are fine careers with rewarding futures but I just wanted them to consider all the options available to them. Nevertheless, I sympathised with the pressure they were under and I appreciated the fact that parents insisted that their children should choose careers in engineering or law. I grew up around kids whose parents did not give a toss about academic pursuits. My own father was none too impressed when I told him that I was going to university but, in the next breath, admitted that he had almost cried when my younger brother scored a great volley in a Sunday league match. Now, if that is not a cultural irony, then I do not know what is.

In fact, my own upbringing helps to explain why I was so insistent that my drama students considered other career options. When I left primary school, my report book read 'Neil has a gift for drama'. If I recall correctly, I had co-written two plays, directed one of them and performed in both by the age of eleven. We also did a reworking of *The Wizard of Oz*. I played the part of Scarecrow and the sizeable audience was treated to the sight of an anorexic beanpole with an uneven haircut performing a song and dance routine. Not bad for a young lad brought up in one of the worst boroughs in the country, academically speaking. However, the next time I did anything remotely dramatic was when I read for a part for some ridiculously pretentious play at university.

My secondary schooldays went by without so much as a dramatic whimper. You see, in my working-class world, the only people who did any sort of acting or singing were homosexuals. Wearing make-up and pretending to be someone else on stage meant that you were gay and you risked social castration. I hate to say it but many of my peers and their families were so prehistoric back then that you could be a bricklayer when you left school and command serious respect but you could not dress up and deliver a few lines.

Consequently, I have been a part of two cultures in which many people just do not get the point of the arts. In England, for example, I only went to the cinema for two reasons. When I was young, it was to ogle beautiful young girls. When I was older, it was so I had a place to kiss average-looking girls.

In Singapore, as we all know, people like to go to the cinema so they have a quiet place to answer their telephone calls. Just as the on-screen killer is about to pounce, you hear 'Hallo, what you want, ah? No lah, cannot. I'm watching movie one. No, cannot what. Show damn good. Yeah, after show, can. We go for makan. Can, no problem.' Before you get a chance to think, you have already turned around and said, 'Look you little prat, if the movie's that good, why don't you just turn your fucking bright yellow handphone off? Second, a "show" is something like a circus that has elephants and live performers jumping around. We, however, are watching a series of moving pictures projected onto that large screen, hence the word "movie".' Well, honestly.

When handphones are not beeping all over the place in the cinema, you can be sure that those stupid red laser pointers are being flashed all over the screen. A couple of years back, my friends and I went to see *The Crucible*, a film I had been waiting to see for some time as I like the work of both Arthur Miller and Daniel Day Lewis. The opening titles had barely gone up when the red laser appeared. Before you knew it, the red spot was tickling Lewis's ear, going up actresses' noses and generally being really boring. No one in the auditorium seemed to find the prank even mildly amusing and I was really losing my temper when I heard 'For fuck's sake, turn it off.' I turned to my friends, who were all staring at me with horrified expressions on their faces. That was when the penny dropped and I realised that the voice must have belonged to me. Momentarily humiliated, a round of applause at the back of the cinema lifted my spirits and I am delighted to say that the red laser was not seen again.

The bottom line is that the arts have not yet acquired the kind of social status that they have in other parts of the world. As long as local universities continue to plug their technological and scientific (money making) degrees, sports and the arts will continue to take a back seat. Watch any play at Victoria Theatre and you will invariably meet young actors and directors outside the building trying to hand you flyers and desperately encouraging you to come down and support their next production. These are the Singaporeans that I truly admire. They appreciate that the buzz that comes from audience applause cannot be matched on a balance sheet. Along the way, they have probably had arguments with relatives over their career choice but these guys have persevered and they are

Singapore's only chance of creating a so-called funky town.

Until that day happens, Singaporeans are going to have to continue to live with certain things. They will still have to rely on the West or Japan for their entertainment, be it on the stage, in the cinema or on the Walkman. There will always be a dearth of artistic talent as long as Singaporeans are encouraged to be stockbrokers or personal bankers. Artists in Singapore should not have to beg you to come and watch their performances nor should they have to tell you to switch off all irritating electronic devices once you are inside the theatre or cinema. But they do. And I cannot see this changing until there is a mindset shift and Singaporeans begin to see a career in the arts as something that can be emotionally rewarding.

The same can be said for sports. No parent can guarantee that their son will grow up to be the next Fandi Ahmad so it is much safer to play the percentages and send him into the corporate world of large salaries and fixed bonuses. When these 'safe' corporate citizens return home, they can switch on their televisions and watch real winners like Manchester United, the Los Angeles Lakers or Pete Sampras, or perhaps they will watch a Hollywood movie and add a few dollars to one of Tom Cruise's bank accounts.

In fact, most Singaporeans were probably doing one of the above on a glorious night back in 1998 when, against all odds, Singapore won its first national soccer trophy, beating Vietnam 1-0 in the Tiger Cup final. I sat on the edge of my seat for 90 minutes. When the final whistle was blown, I ran around the room cheering. I felt privileged that I had somehow been a part of Singaporean sporting history. I was the only one cheering, though. When England scored against Germany in the 1996 European championship semi-final, you could hear the whole street celebrating in Dagenham. However, here, I was in an HDB block with common corridors and I did not hear a thing. I went out into the corridor to overhear the television sets and the majority were switched to one of those period dramas, with lots of kung fu fighting and crying. Hardly anyone was watching the final. It must have been assumed that Singapore had forgotten how to win a football match. Now that they had, no one was really interested. To me it was a really deflating, anticlimactic realisation, a bit like being smacked on the jaw by a man who supports the same team as you. It became obvious that sports, like the arts, are considered something that you do at school or play occasionally to keep fit but neither are considered viable career options. All the Tiger Cup wins in the world will not change that. Depressing? It is enough to turn you into a personal banker but, please God, don't.

Chapter Thirteen

Scott was given seven days to leave Singapore. Just a day after he had opened his first bank account and a month after he had moved into his own room with a lovely Indian family, he was ordered to clear off back to England. We were both devastated. When I returned from work that Saturday night, I was shocked to find Scott and our friend Victor sitting on Saudita's sofa. Scott broke the silence saying, 'Immigration has told me to fuck off. I've got until the end of the week. The bastards.'

I could not begin to imagine how he felt. To plant firm roots in a country, only to have them mercilessly ripped out by an anonymous bureaucrat must be soul-destroying. The poor sod told me he stepped out of the immigration building and started to cry. What else could he do? All his plans and ambitions for the next couple of years had been crushed by one man's 'no'. On top of this, Immigration is not obliged to give a reason for rejecting work permit applications so it did not. I know that Scott is just a number to them, a name on a piece of paper, but a 'sorry' would have been nice rather than something along the lines of 'Sod off. We do not want you here. We accept that you've just moved into a new apartment with a lovely Indian family and have paid out over

S$1,000 in rent and deposits but tough shit. As for the reasons for rejecting you, even though your work record is exemplary, we do not have to give them so we will not. Goodbye.'

That is water under the bridge now and Scott has not looked back. The silly sod is now working for an up-and-coming architect's practice in Central London. He has also married a beautiful girl from Wales. Make no mistake; he has come back with a vengeance. However, he is still prone to the odd cock-up from time to time.

There is a London gangster movie called *Villain* that I absolutely love. Set in 1970, the movie stars the great Richard Burton as a sadistic gang boss. When I heard it had been re-released in England, I asked Scott to send me a copy and he kindly obliged. Then came the cock-up.

One morning, I received a card from the Singapore Board of Film Censors informing me that a package had arrived for me and requesting that I go down to their offices for a little chat. It turned out that Scott, the dopey but honest soul, had carelessly noted that the contents of the package contained a video. Therefore, the parcel had been re-routed to the Board.

I have always abhorred censorship so I knew that I might say something that my employment pass would later regret. As a precaution, I took Greg, my old boss and good friend, with me. Now Greg is as cool as they come and I suspected I might need to exercise his calm diplomatic skills and possibly his knowledge of other local languages. When we arrived at the offices of the Board of Film Censors, the guy at the counter produced my package and explained that he could open it only in my presence. Reluctantly, I agreed and surprise, surprise it was my movie from Scott. The guy then highlighted my 'options'. I had the right to return the parcel to its sender, settling the issue on the spot. Alternatively, I could *pay* the Board to kindly view the film for me. The Board would then decide what was suitable viewing for *me* and I would have to pay them again if any cuts were made.

True to form, I completely lost it. 'Are you telling me that guys in this building, who have never met me, are going to decide what I can watch?'

'Yes.'

'Wait a minute. This is a gift from a close friend. How would you feel if one of your close friends sent you a gift, only for me to intercept it? I then open it and inform you that a stranger is going to examine it to decide which parts you can have. A service for which you have to pay. How would you feel?'

'You can just send it back if you like.'

'But it's a gift. My friend has taken the trouble to send it. Why the hell would I want to send it back?'

'In that case, you can have it viewed by the Board. Here are the charges.' He then gave me a leaflet containing all the charges. It was so many dollars per 30 minutes and then a couple of dollars per cut. It was insane.

'I've never heard of this policy. I know films are censored but I didn't know you had a policy like this,' I argued back.

'Would you like to send the film back?'

'No, it's my bloody film. I don't see why I have to pay you to cut it for me.'

'Those are your options.'

'I didn't know about them, though. It's not as if these leaflets are available in supermarkets or in MRT stations, is it?'

We were going around in circles so Greg intervened, 'I think there's a lack of awareness here. My friend hasn't been in Singapore for very long so perhaps it would be worth considering the idea that such material be made more readily available for foreign workers at airports and at immigration. This would be in the best interests of both parties and episodes like this could then be avoided.' He was not saying anything radical but it deflated the situation a little.

'I'll pass on your feedback,' came the quick, diplomatic reply.

'That's still not going to help me, is it?' came the even speedier retort.

I knew I was fighting a losing battle so I took a calculated gamble and lost. 'Okay, I'll pay you to watch my gift. I've watched the film dozens of times and I've seen more violence on a Channel 8 kung fu "family" drama. I'm convinced there's absolutely nothing you'll find worth cutting,' I said confidently.

When I collected my film a week later, it had two cuts and I received a bill for around S$10. It was impossible to fathom what scenes in the movie could be deemed cut-worthy. However, I was presented with a cute little censor information card, detailing the cuts and why they had been administered. Only a thoroughbred civil servant could have written the card. I have still got it somewhere and it says something like 'Cut number 1, 58th minute, lady exposing both breasts.' I burst out laughing. They are certainly taking the business of fun seriously down at the Censors Board.

The lady in question was exposing not one but, shock horror, both breasts. If she had only exposed one of her breasts, perhaps the cut would have been half as long. The Board was right, of course, but it was such a trivial breast showing incident that I had forgotten all about it. Prior to beating a guy senseless in a men's toilet (which is, of course, acceptable), Burton chats with the victim in a strip bar while a topless belly dancer is doing her thing in the background. Thus, I will put my hands up here and admit that I had missed that one. I had completely forgotten that you are permitted to watch a man be savagely beaten on the silver screen, a gruesome scene that I have been lucky enough never to witness in my life, but you cannot watch a woman baring something as natural as her breasts, a quite wonderful scene that I have been lucky enough to witness twice in my life.

The second cut just knocked my socks off. Part of the scene in which Burton chats to his victim in the strip bar was cut. Why? Well, as the card says: 'Poster on wall in background has pictures of women exposing breasts.' The card did not go so far as to say whether the women were exposing both of their breasts but I suppose it is serious enough when more than one woman is involved. Now excuse my uncensored language but these people need to get a fucking life. Despite the number of times I had previously watched the film in England, I had never noticed the poster. Who on earth is censoring and cutting our movies? Have they ever been with a woman before? If they have not, I have a shocking revelation to make – women have breasts. Admittedly, they come in all shapes and sizes but women nonetheless have them. Why Singaporean film censors are hell-bent on denying their existence is a mystery to me. And let's be brutally honest here. I know for a fact that you can see the real thing for almost the price of a movie ticket at any of the brothels in Geylang so what is the bloody point?

Calming down a little, my foray into immigration and censorship is my long-winded way of coming round to the subject of politics and government. The reason being, as I hope I have made clear, you can feel the hand of the Singaporean government everywhere. An inevitable reality perhaps when you consider that we are living in what is essentially a one-party state. However, before anyone panics, namely civil servants and my publisher, I am not about to turn this book into a political treatise. I have no intention of writing an academic text on the nature of Singapore's government largely because so many other writers (i.e., Singaporeans) could do a far better job. Besides, I have more positive things to say about this government than I do negative, which may surprise many people.

My formative years of studying history had taught me that Singapore was a trading post for the British, founded by that fella whose name is now shared with the hotel where you get the famous cocktail. Interestingly enough, the British prime minister at that time was one Lord Liverpool. Now wouldn't it be marvellous if hotels, streets, airport lounges, MRT stations and goodness knows what else here were named after him? That would really make my day if the thousands of local Manchester United fans had to go into the Liverpool bar in Liverpool Street next to Liverpool Place station to watch their Devils play.

I soon realised that knowledge of the East India Company, British imperialism and nineteenth-century trading routes was not heavily sought after in Singaporean coffee shop conversations. I also accepted that I could only take the Lord Liverpool joke so far, although he did have a foreign secretary called Lord Castlereagh who engineered the settlement after the Napoleonic Wars and then went and slit his own throat in front of a mirror. This, of course, has no relevance except for the fact that I use any excuse to tell that story. Consequently, I knew that I needed to brush up on my knowledge of this modern metropolis.

Reading through travel books, I kept stumbling across the term 'soft authoritarianism'. Western writers wrote of 'subservient', even 'cowed', Singaporeans who always did what they were told.

Democratic elections were a formality as the People's Action Party had been returned to power with huge majorities on every occasion since June 1959. Lee Kuan Yew was the youngest prime minister in the world at that time and when he chose to step down in 1990, he had become one of the longest-serving party leaders in modern leadership. I then discovered that one of his sons, Lee Hsien Loong, was deputy prime minister. Well, this sounded like a fun, Orwellian place to be with an all-powerful nepotistic government.

Consequently, I was completely opposed to the Singaporean government for about two months after my arrival. I was totally appalled by the seemingly infinite number of fines that the government had introduced for what appeared to be such minor misdemeanours. For example, there are penalties for not flushing toilets, littering, eating or drinking on any form of public transport and jaywalking. Both Scott and I could not believe that such draconian measures were still being implemented and, more importantly, enforced in this day and age. I was becoming quite depressed by it all so I asked Justyn, an expatriate friend who had lived in Singapore for a number of years, if he believed that Singapore was an authoritarian state.

He said, 'Well, look at it this way. What is there that you can't do? You can earn a decent living but you are not allowed to commit crimes. Really, there's not a great deal that you can't do except for the things you shouldn't want to do.'

I slowly began to agree with him. I have learnt to accept and agree with the majority of Singapore's harsh laws. The obvious retort to this is that I have lived in the country too long and have fallen for the rhetoric. On the contrary, it was living on a working-class council estate for almost twenty years that changed my mind. It became an absolute joy to walk down streets that were not strewn with litter, dog shit and chewing gum that sticks to your shoes and requires the services of a welder to remove.

When I first returned to England for a holiday over the Christmas period, I found myself complaining like a grumpy old man. There was litter everywhere and teenagers were still hanging out on street corners, only their language had become cruder. The local newspaper could print nothing other than murders, muggings, burglaries and demands for increased welfare benefits for Dagenham's high population of teenage mothers. Sure, I could step into any store and buy an uncensored movie but why would I bother? There was plenty of sex and violence in my former home town to keep me entertained. Ironically, the setting up of closed circuit television (CCTV) cameras just about everywhere confirmed that there was a 'Big Brother' world after all. Fortunately, I had left it to live in Singapore.

So what are some of the so-called draconian laws enforced by the Singaporean government? Western travel writers constantly bemoan the fact that Singapore is a 'fine' city and tourists even buy the 'Singapore's a "fine" city' T-shirts that mock all the things that cannot be done here. To me, this is such a naive perception. At the end of the day, if you think that the fines are ridiculously steep (for example, around S$1,000 for littering), then the simple solution is not to break the laws in the first place. I will not apologise if I sound like an eighteenth-century Tory here. Singapore is spotless and it has some of the cleanest public amenities I have ever seen; a fact that is all the more impressive when you consider its high population density.

When I was growing up, I had the misfortune of needing to visit the little boy's room urgently on several occasions and had no choice but to use the ones found in London Underground train stations. The foul stench numbed the sinuses on entry. Graffiti was everywhere and, in some instances, it seemed marker pens were not readily available so the artist had managed to 'produce' a different kind of writing material. Unsurprisingly, there was hardly ever any soap in the dispensers and as for finding any toilet paper, well, you had more chance of bumping into George Michael. In Singapore, of course, all of the above offences would carry fines, but most public facilities are rarely abused or mistreated. Funny, that, when you think about it.

Please do not think for a second that England is a lawless society, far from it. The home secretary has got laws coming out of every orifice. These laws, however, are not enforced in the same way. That is the crucial difference. Being caught on the train or the tube without a valid ticket in England makes you liable for an on-the-spot £10 fine (about S$25). In Singapore, on the other hand, if the ticket inspector finds you without a valid ticket, he will usually take your farecard and charge S$1 to it (just 40 pence).

When I was a teenager, I needed to get a train to and from school. I always had my train fare but I would more often than not spend the money on something else and sneak through the station without paying. Looking back, this was, sad to say, probably as easy as it sounds. All you had to do was evade the eyes of one guy. That was it. One guy, who was usually overweight, would sit in his little glass cubicle and you would flash your school pass or your daily ticket at him and walk past. It was such an easy, low-paid job and most of the time the guy only gave a token glance up at the hundreds of blurred tickets that whizzed past him. Still, when I was thirteen years old, it seemed like Mission Impossible.

Of course, it was wrong to evade paying my fare and thus break the law, but it was so easy. If I was caught, I would just tell the man that I had made the shortest journey possible and give him 30 pence to pacify him. Officially, he was supposed to hand all monies in but when he walked home, he could play the tune of 'Jingle Bells' without moving his lips. That was how it was in England, just about everyone broke the law on British Rail.

Now, there are ticket barriers at the entrance and exit of each train station, while London Underground has gone one step further and installed CCTV cameras and alarm barriers that can only be opened with a valid ticket inside every tube station. Have these improved the system? What do you think? Little laws have been broken for so long that there is now no turning back.

Coming home on the tube a couple of years ago, I watched dumbstruck as two kids jumped over the barriers and walked off without showing their tickets. They did this under the watchful eye of the CCTV cameras and in front of commuters and the on-duty station officer. The boys made no attempt to run and no one, including me, dared to stop them. Life is just too short. I would have lacked the balls to carry out such an act of bravado at their age. Then it occurred to me. They were roughly the age I was when I used to carry out my Mission Impossible routine. The obstacles might have changed but the crime remains the same. Both they and I have been conditioned by an environment in which laws are rarely enforced. And as for that seemingly draconian on-the-spot £10 fine? Flummoxed Metropolitan police officers are continually being given false names and have to spend thousands of pounds of taxpayers' money to track down the offenders to retrieve the fines.

Singapore, on the other hand, enforces its laws and is not afraid to mete out punishment. Admittedly, the size of the island certainly aids law enforcement as criminals are not exactly overwhelmed with a choice of safe houses. If you rob a petrol station, expect imprisonment. If you commit rape, expect imprisonment and the cane. If you commit a murder or bring heroin into the country, expect the rope. To middle-class Western academics, who tend to live in little suburbs with white picket fences and are very quick to criticise Singapore's stance on crime without actually living here, my retort is simple: do not break the law. I know what to expect, Singaporeans know what to expect and Michael Fay knew what to expect.

In 1994, the American teenager achieved global fame when he was given four months imprisonment and four strokes of the cane for vandalising cars. Like many expatriates here, he obviously had too much time on his hands and was soon bored with the kind of luxuries that the Singaporean kids living in my HDB block can only dream of. The spoilt brat deserved everything he got. After all, I do not like everything about Singapore but if I am content to take home its dollars every month, then I have to accept certain things like having my video censored for me. Similarly, Fay's family had to accept that 'when in Rome', they cannot behave how they please, safe in the knowledge that Uncle Sam will come in and save the day.

After doing a search on the Internet for Michael Fay-related sites, I was quite surprised to find that he did not have too many sympathisers. In fact, one or two Americans even applauded the no-nonsense and no-exception policy of the Singaporean government. After all, if its lawmakers chose, quite correctly, not to spare the life of Filipina maid Flor Contemplacion after she was found guilty of two murders in 1991, why the hell should they spare some irritating American adolescent from a few strokes of the cane?

Of course, the Singaporean government is not perfect and sometimes its leading ministers make pronouncements that send me reeling in disbelief. There are just two areas that really rankle with me: censorship and homosexuality.

I have absolutely no problem with being hanged if I import heroin or being fined S$1,000 for dropping an ATM receipt. However, I do have a major problem with being told what I can and cannot watch at the cinema, on stage or even in the privacy of my own home. In our so-called New Economy, any form of censorship is going to be pretty much redundant. It was no secret that when the movie *Titanic* was released, Singaporeans were watching it over the Net to see the uncensored scenes of the actress lying naked on a couch.

The technological age is progressing so rapidly that the laws on censorship seem like an anachronism of the previous century when, perhaps, they had more validity. I can understand how ultra left-wing movies might have caused problems in the 1960s or films criticising neighbouring countries and trading partners might not have gone down well in the 1980s but what is there to fear now? If I am missing the point somewhere, it really does not matter because Singaporeans can access those 'fearful' things on the Net anyway.

Now do not assume that I escaped censorship just because I grew up in a Western society. I was raised during the Thatcher years; a time when former British agents had their books about spycatching banned in their own country and the national tabloid, the *Sun*, selected our government for us. Therefore, I am no stranger to a little censorship and manipulation but that does not mean that I will condone it.

Ironically, the funniest part about censorship is that as soon as something is banned, everybody wants it. It is basic human nature. Watching Singaporean friends distribute chewing gum excitedly after a trip to Malaysia is painfully embarrassing to watch. In my last job, colleagues would leave messages on the staff noticeboard informing us that they had a box of chewing gum. Before you could say 'It's just a stick of gum that cannot be swallowed and looks like a small brain when you've finished chewing it', everyone was diving into the box.

Just recently, I watched the movie *Me, Myself and Irene*, which was a gross bodily-function affair. What was really irritating about the film was that the local censors allowed all of the gross scenes to stay but omitted some of the funniest dialogues in the movie. That is, the fast-talking jive between three young black actors because, I assume, of the word 'motherfucker'. I am not saying that it is not an unpleasant word but is it any worse than watching a man (and a dog) defecating on a lawn?

This highlights the fundamental problem I have with any form of censorship. It is determined by the opinions of a small group of strangers. Just because they are upstanding and usually wealthy and successful members of the community, what right do they have to tell me what I can watch and hear? Whether it is Frankie Goes To Hollywood's 'Relax', which was not allowed radio play in Britain at one time, or Oliver Stone's *Natural Born Killers*, which was banned in Singapore, if I am not allowed to hear or see either of them, then I am left with one radical course of action – to switch on my computer and click my mouse. The ability to disseminate information has progressed so rapidly that continuing to censor artistic performances seems about as ridiculous as me paying a man to open up and cut a gift that was addressed to me. Therefore, I suspect that the laws on censorship will change over the next decade or so before they become redundant.

But I do not suspect that views on homosexuality will change. I have a close friend, a Singaporean accountant, who is gay. He shares a wonderful relationship with his mother but he can never tell her that he is gay. He fears it would break her heart and she would never speak to him again. He suspects the same reaction from his father. When he told me, I was disgusted and shocked because he bore no resentment to either parent. 'That is just the way it is,' he said. Due to these deep-rooted values, my friend has to spend the rest of his life living a lie not only to his society but also to his own parents. What does that have to do with the PAP?

Well, it is true that conservatism breeds conservatism. But which came first? A politically-apathetic, traditional society of Singaporeans or a repressive government? I do not know the answer and I do not care. All I know is that I do not see people on the streets demanding freedom of expression or equality for gays. Can a people be that easily afraid or, more depressingly, that easily bought off? Whatever the reason, many Singaporeans give the impression of being conservative. As I write this, a number of letters appeared in the *Straits Times* Forum pages demanding the *Harry Potter* series of children's books be banned on the grounds that they dabble with the occult. If any of those letter writers read this, highly unlikely as they are probably attending a neo-Nazi book burning rally, can I please say 'Get a life.' As one sensible Singaporean retorted, *The Wizard of Oz* deals with witches and wizards as does *The Chronicles of Narnia* so should we ban them as well? While we are at it, Enid Blyton wrote about elves and shoemakers while Roald Dahl wrote a book about some witches and it was a comedy. How dare he, the bastard. Now with Singaporeans like these, who needs soft authoritarianism?

It does not stop there. In a quite tragic incident, a girl was killed in 2000 when a plant pot fell from an HDB block and hit her on the head as she walked beneath the block. It was a sad, million-to-one tragedy. Nevertheless, it happened and the government was right to take action. Residents in my block do leave objects, such as pots and prayer objects, hanging precariously over the edges of window sills and ledges and these objects are undoubtedly dangerous. After the incident, the HDB and Town Councils stipulated that a written warning would be issued to any resident storing 'killer litter' and if the resident did not take heed of the warning, further steps would be taken. That seemed the rational approach to take. For some, however, it was not enough. There were public demands for residents to be evicted or to have their flat confiscated if found guilty. I found myself laughing at the insanity of it all. By all means, fine residents but to take away their S$400,000 property and leave them homeless for hanging a plant pot on a window ledge seems a trifle excessive. Once again, the demand had come from below and not from above.

Almost every Singaporean over thirty that I know, in some cases younger, has no great desire to see censorship abolished or homosexuality legalised. If they do, they are certainly not going to risk their status and financial security to bring it about. I know of gay doctors who are not happy with the status quo but do not want to risk their standard of living to change it. Maybe Singaporeans have been bought after all and Lee Kuan Yew, after looking at the political and economic turmoil in the region over the last couple of years, really does understand his voters. If you had grown up in a kampung but now had a home, a car, a steady income, an annual holiday and could provide a decent education for your children, what is a little censorship and homophobia?

Of course, not every Singaporean in the twenty-first century grew up in a kampung. Younger Singaporeans are becoming more aware of societies that have greater artistic and sexual freedom. This, I feel, is the greatest threat to the future of the Singaporean government. Cleanliness, safety, efficiency and strong moral values may be able to retain the likes of me, simply because I have already had a bellyful of the alternative, but these guys have experienced nothing else. And it is going to take more than a Speaker's Corner, which could end up just attracting tourists like the one in London's Hyde Park, to keep them here. An increasingly intelligent, knowledge-based population, which is what the government wants, may feel restricted and somewhat insulted if they can make big bucks during the day but cannot cuddle up with the partner of their choice and watch uncensored films by night. It is a compromising situation that will be enough to retain the greedy, kiasu brigade but it will not be enough to keep those few talents who view life as something more than just accumulating dollars.

So let's remove the shackles on the arts scene and have a few laughs. Allow actors to speak Singlish, crack a few jokes, be homosexual, play football or do whatever they like if it is all in the name of realistic performance. If a young couple is madly in love, let them walk down the street hand in hand, whether they be two men, two women or even a pair of American tourists. None of these changes can be considered particularly radical today and I am positive that it will not lead to the government being toppled.

Aside from my old secondary school's sixth form committee, over which I happened to be the chairman, there is no such thing as a perfect government. However, for my money, the PAP does okay. It guarantees a standard of living that few countries in the world can match. It has no welfare, which keeps taxes low, yet its educational and medical facilities are heavily subsidised and affordable to almost everyone. And unlike many British governments, its members do not have the habit of being found in uncompromising positions with hookers and independent auditors. No government can ever be completely secure in its position but the PAP comes fairly close. So if it could just open up on issues pertaining to sex, freedom of speech and artistic expression, something that the Net is doing anyway, then it might plug that brain drain.

While it is at it, perhaps the government could introduce a law that stipulates all public servants must smile and answer their telephones or risk imprisonment. And if the government could also deport on sight any tourist found wearing white, knee-high socks with sandals, then Singaporeans could truly say that they have never had it so good.

Chapter Fourteen

I suppose it was a Caucasian dressed as a banana and giving away cocktails that drew us to the place. We needed a bar to celebrate one of our colleagues leaving and this particular one looked ideal. Tucked away in a little side street off Orchard Road, it was directly opposite where we worked. The majority of its clientele were Caucasians, or ang mohs. This is hardly surprising as the banana at the door was giving away delicious banana cocktails to anyone who entered. Most of the ang mohs I know (myself included) will walk barefoot over broken glass to get at cheap drinks. Our party that night all agreed with banana man that this was the place to be.

It was almost a classic night. Scott and I drank so many banana cocktails that we could have been peeled by the end of the evening. Everything was going along swimmingly and we all promised to be the best of friends until the end of time. Then everything went pear-shaped. There was a group of obnoxious blokes in their forties who began to make some lewd comments to some of the ladies in our group. It culminated with one guy leaning over to my missus and saying he liked her so much he intended to 'put his hand up her skirt'. Things became a little hysterical after that and an excellent evening was thoroughly spoilt.

So allow me to ask you a question. Bearing in mind that both Singaporeans and Caucasians were in the bar, who were the cavemen that night? I must have been in dozens of Singaporean bars and nightclubs and things have only ever got heated twice. On both occasions, they involved ang mohs. On that particular night, the trouble was caused by a group of Australian tourists who were determined to intimidate as many people as possible. When informed that my partner was not only seeing someone but that he was standing opposite her in the bar, the Aussie Neanderthal replied, 'Good.' It just warms the heart, doesn't it?

Apart from skin colour, I have nothing in common with these Caucasians. To be honest, I have very little in common with the expatriates who live in Singapore either. For a start, most of the ang mohs that live here, particularly the ones from Britain, tend to come from the upper-middle classes. Singaporean employers are not going to search the far reaches of London, New York and Paris to find road sweepers and table attendants when there are plenty of poor souls from India and the Philippines that they can offer crap wages to instead. Second, ang mohs here are highly-skilled in line with Singapore's 'foreign talent' policy. Sorry, I mean 'global talent' policy.

Highly trained for nothing when I first arrived, the global talent policy was about as useful to me as a pair of sunglasses to a man with one ear. With large broking firms unimpressed by my ability to highlight the differences between Stalinism and Nazism, I began to seriously resent those ang mohs strutting around the business district with their briefcases, handphones and Brylcreamed hair. As I sat on a bench overlooking the Singapore River in a pair of Bermuda shorts and flip-flops and eating Scott's cheese slice sandwiches, it became obvious that I had more in common with the local guys who drank Tiger beer in my Toa Payoh coffee shop. The snotty-nosed guys called Arthur and Charles, whom I had so despised at university, had arrived in Singapore in their thousands to earn big bucks and live in condos with swimming pools. Call it jealousy or envy, call it whatever you bloody like, but I could not bring myself to like them. Almost immediately, Scott and I began to distinguish 'us' from 'them'. If I was asked to accurately define 'them', I probably could not. All I can say is, just hang out at, say, Holland Village, Clarke Quay or any coffee bar around Orchard Road and you will see them and their tourist brothers and sisters everywhere.

The funniest part is that if you happen to be in a lift or a train carriage with one of them, they treat you like a long-lost colonial cousin; a fellow son of Mother England, keeping a stiff upper lip in the face of unknown Asian adversities. They seem to believe that there is a shared British bond, or a subconscious connection, that is somehow going to turn us into instant friends. Now there would be nothing wrong with this if it was not for the fact that these very same people used to walk past me in their thousands as I travelled to work each day in London. When I was a lowly temp working at Britain's top stockbroking firm, there were colleagues sitting opposite my desk who did not even know my name. Put these people on a train in Singapore and suddenly they want to share their life history with me.

My girlfriend and I were coming home from work together once when we were collared. Both being teachers at that time, we were discussing our classes when a guy resembling Charles Manson came over.

Straight to the point, he asked, 'So you're both teachers here then?'

'Erm, that's right,' I replied cautiously, acutely aware that half of the carriage was listening to us as ang mohs, particularly Americans, have a tendency to converse loudly in public places.

'Oh, I thought so. I overheard you taking about it.'

'Really? Are you a teacher as well?' I asked politely. At this point, my partner shot me a filthy look. She has barely enough patience to sustain a conversation with me, let alone one with a complete stranger.

'I was. Weren't we all? Ha ha. I taught English as a foreign language in Spain and I did it here for a while too. What else can "we" do here? Ha ha.'

Well, 'we' could keep our voices down a little, I thought. But he had no intention of letting up.

'Then I travelled the world a bit. Well, you've got to, haven't you? While you've the chance, that is. How long have you been here then?'

'On this train? About ten minutes.'

This puzzled Charles. 'No, I meant how long have you been in Singapore?'

'Oh, I see. About six months now. Oh, Toa Payoh. This is our stop. It was nice talking to you.'

'Yes, you too. So you live here do you?'

'No, we live in an apartment just around the corner.'

'What? Oh I see. Well, take care. Maybe I'll see you around. Bye.' The doors closed and Charles disappeared into the night.

I was twenty-two when I had that conversation and it was the longest I had ever had with a British stranger. Yet I had to come all the way to Singapore for it to happen.

Of course, the conversations are not always as long as that. We were having a barbecue at a friend's condominium once and I got into the lift to get some charcoal from his flat. An ang moh also got in the lift, spotted the S-League football shirt that I was wearing and got quite excited about it.

'So you're a professional footballer over here, are you? That must be exciting. Which team do you play for? I expect the money's good, isn't it?'

'Sorry, I'm not a footballer. I'm a teacher. I just wear this for fun, mate,' I replied.

'Oh, sorry. I thought you were a footballer out here.' He was visibly crestfallen.

'Are you a footballer?' I asked cheerily.

'No, I'm not,' he replied miserably.

'Oh well, that's settled then. I'm off to get some charcoal. Bye.'

It is not only strangers who act in this manner. Even my mother somehow expects the Brits abroad to stick together. When Nick Leeson, the rogue trader who almost destroyed Barings Bank, was imprisoned here at Changi Prison, my mother telephoned me.

'Hello mate,' she began innocently, 'have you heard the news?'

'Did Gary get that promotion?'

'No, have you heard about poor old Nick Leeson.'

'Nick Leeson? No, what's happening? Are they releasing him?'

'No. They say he's dying from cancer. He's been moved to the prison hospital.'

'Really? That's a shame, isn't it?'

There was a slight pause on the other end of the line before she asked, 'Well?'

'Well, what?'

'Well, can't you visit him or something? He is British and he probably hasn't got many friends out there. If you visit him, it might cheer him up a bit.'

Now this sounded ridiculous. I might respect the guy and sympathise with his predicament. After all, any working-class bloke who almost single-handedly brings down an archaic, nepotistic crappy old institution is all right by me. As for me strolling into a prison hospital with a bunch of flowers to chat with him, just because he happened to be born on the same island as me, is taking things a little too far.

I tried to explain this to my mum. 'But I don't even know him, do I? I have more in common with my next-door neighbours. They keep an eye on our apartment when we're on holiday and we give them clothes for their nieces and nephews. What have I got in common with Nick Leeson?'

'He's a Brit.'

'So are thousands of people in the hospitals around London and they don't all have people to look after them but we don't worry about them.'

'All right, all right... Oh, by the way, Gary got the promotion. He's in charge now.' She did not mention Leeson ever again.

Shortly after that conversation, the former trader was released from prison and returned to Britain. I sincerely hope he recovers and makes as much money as he possibly can out of the wonderful Barings Bank incident. I can safely say, though, that I do not expect us to be on each other's Christmas card list this year.

I suppose it is because I fall under the Hon school of thought. Hon is a Cantonese guy who lived on our corridor in the halls of residence at university. Unlike many of his friends, he refused to join the Hong Kong Society. When Scott asked him why, he replied, 'If I wanted to hang around with people from Hong Kong, I might as well have stayed in Hong Kong.' We liked him immediately.

I have to say that I agree with Hon's profoundly simple outlook on travel and cultural exploration. It is no coincidence that I have more local friends in Singapore than I do Caucasian. With over four million of the former, and only a few hundred thousand of the latter, how could it be any other way? In fact, I would have to actually go out of my way to seek ang mohs to hang out with. Surely no one is going to do that, are they? But of course they are. That is why I cannot blame local friends when they introduce me to expats thinking that I will be grateful because that is what all the others seem to be doing. Have a look for yourself. Go to any Western-style bar and you will see white people drinking with more white people. Alternatively, take a tetanus injection and have a cultural encounter at the legendary Papa Jo's nightspot in Orchard Road. Like vampires, the ang moh crowd comes out at night, dressed in their best shirts and armed with plenty of tax-free Singapore dollars to woo those local darlings tragically struck down by the Pinkerton syndrome. Like the character in Madame Butterfly, they are somehow lured by the attraction of drunken voices and the possibility of a fat wallet.

Many of the expats I come across merely uproot their Western lifestyle and replant it here. Go to any hawker centre in the HDB heartlands and play a game of 'spot the white man'. To be honest, you would have better odds if you went over to Pulau Ubin and played 'spot the tiger'. However, your chances of success would skyrocket if you played the same game at any French-style sandwich outlet. And what is it about these places anyway? Am I alone in thinking that the food is dry, bland and far too expensive? My mother makes more exciting sandwiches and rolls and she does not have to wear those sad, unrealistic French maid aprons while she is doing it.

I went into one of these Western hellholes in International Plaza once in a bid to tackle a raging thirst. As it was lunchtime, the place was heaving with city-slickers. Saying hello to the Chinese auntie behind the counter, I was greeted with the kind of facial expression that suggested I had just vomited on her counter. I picked up a can of warm diet coke and asked her the price.

'$1.70,' she replied, without even looking up. Momentarily stunned, I thought she had said S$1.70 so I asked her the price again. My ears were not deceiving me.

'Excuse me, do you inject bacardi into it or something? Only it's not even cold and I'm taking it away so it won't even come with ice.'

'It's $1.70.'

I threw the can at her silly apron and walked out. Approximately five metres away was a little hawker stall. The cheerful Chinese uncle sold me a cold can of coke for S$1, asked if I wanted a straw and said goodbye. His stall, though doing a thriving trade, did not have a single ang moh around it.

It does not stop there. I have ang moh friends who refuse to set foot in a hawker centre, who drink in Western-style pubs and only eat Western food. Their wives stay at home and perform the dutiful role of housewife. They sit by the swimming pool or watch videos of English soap operas or dramas that they have either rented from the British Council or had sent out to them by relatives. Their children go to international schools and mix predominantly with other rich white children. After work, they drink in coffee shops in Western-style areas like Holland Village. In other words, there is little attempt to acclimatise to the local way of life. They live in a cocoon, a Western bubble of condos, cars, maids, cable television, bars and restaurants, thus ensuring they have only minimal contact with the average Singaporean and his way of life. Such a self-centred lifestyle can only further exacerbate the idea of 'them' and 'us' and make Singaporeans less susceptible to the notion of foreign talent, even if it is euphemistically called global talent.

It infuriates me because I know exactly how Singaporeans must feel. When I was at university, I have to concede that our good friend Hon was very much a minority. The Asians who lived on our corridor brought their little bit of Asia with them. Before you could say haute cuisine, our kitchen was stocked with rice cookers, chopsticks and those huge chicken rice choppers. With the exception of David, I never saw an Asian cook anything mildly resembling a Western meal in three years. Whether they were from Malaysia, Hong Kong, Brunei or Singapore, they always cooked rice and noodles. On top of that, they always cooked together. In fact, they did most things together, such as eating out and going to the cinema. They never came out to the pub or played football with us, no matter how many times we asked them. Such a relationship raises cultural barriers and, after a while, it became a 'them' and 'us' situation, which makes for fraught living conditions.

Ironically, Scott and I were more willing to hang around with the Asians on our corridor than we were with our fellow Caucasians because we were in the middle of our (admittedly childish) class war. In truth, we really did have far more in common with Dave from Toa Payoh than we did with spoilt, rich arseholes from London or York. We would chat about global issues such as Manchester United, Singaporean snakes and pornography. However, we always went our separate ways when it came to going out in the evenings and that inevitably bred a little resentment. They would go off to the Chinese food wholesaler to stock up on rice while we went to the pub to stock up on cider.

Like Hon, though, there are always exceptions. I have many good friends here who have made every effort to assimilate themselves into the culture. In fact, one of my friends, Fran, tried so hard he ended up marrying a Singaporean. Lawrence refused to eat anything Western because it was too expensive and there was too much local food to choose from. Shawn, another friend, who went a little further north and married a Korean girl, enjoyed the company of Singaporeans so much that he would bare his buttocks to them at every opportunity. Why he could not just shake their hand is a mystery to me.

We were having a few drinks at Fran's HDB apartment one night when trousers started being dropped with mind-numbing predictability around midnight. On this particular occasion, Shawn got his wires crossed. After half a bottle of Fran's Chivas Regal, he assumed that Lawrence, who had just mooned him, was in the kitchen. Consequently, Shawn went down on all fours and dropped his trousers to reveal his backside and a little of what can only be called the world's scrawniest chicken. For what seemed like an eternity, he stayed in that position saying things like 'Get a load of that, you bastard.' Only Lawrence was not in the kitchen. He was sitting at the bar with Fran and me, watching this bizarre episode unfold. Fran's wife was in the kitchen preparing some snacks and she saw a side of Ontario that night that I hope she never gets to witness again.

Such drunken buffoonery is uncommon among most Singaporeans. This is because they substitute beer with good food, something that I begrudgingly admire. Eating a delicious plate of *hor fun* may not stimulate the kind of excitable behaviour required to bare your bottom to friends but it will not inspire you to try to put your hand up a complete stranger's skirt either.

Of course, the differences between locals and ang mohs are endless but it is the peculiar ones that intrigue me. In England, for instance, hairdressers like to talk profusely. I knew a gay hairdresser in Manchester who used to cut hair at the local old folks' home and recalled in minute detail all the old ladies who had died in the chair while he was still cutting their hair. He even expressed regret that he had not been paid for the cut. Then, there was the girl in Dagenham who kindly informed me that I had the kind of hair that was impossible to cut and that she could do absolutely nothing with it. At my old Singaporean hairdressers in Toa Payoh, however, they said nothing. Partly because their command of the English language was not the best but mainly because they just could not be bothered. I would walk in, the hairdresser would ask, 'Wha you want...short?' and that would be it. No pleasantries, no chitchat, nothing. If I am in an HDB lift with Singaporeans, they want to know my life story; when I am in a Singaporean hairdresser's chair, he or she wants me to shut up.

The one thing Singaporeans most certainly do not do is scratch their testicles in public. This is in complete contrast to the Western male. I had assumed that it was a British phenomenon connected to the seasonal weather. Then I realised that Canadians, if Fran, Shawn and Lawrence are any yardstick, were also guilty of it. Singaporeans, on the other hand, keep well away from their nether regions. This, to me, demonstrates remarkable self-restraint. In a country that sits on the equator and is humid all year round, I have to ask: how *do* you do it? It is impossible for me *not* to resemble Captain Hook with chickenpox when I am sitting on a non air-conditioned bus in the midday Sun and feel the sweat trickle down my inner thigh.

Somehow though, Singaporeans can resist the temptation to

rip open the underside of their scrotum. Yet strangely, some, particularly the older ones, cannot resist emptying their throat of phlegm whenever the need arises. My next-door neighbour has a spitting session in his bathroom every morning at the same time. His James Brown impressions almost serve as a wake-up call. He saves his best performance for Sunday mornings when he sounds as if he is trying to raise the *Titanic*. I know that spitting is a sensitive issue in Singapore and Caucasians tend to zoom in on it when they pick out negative traits, but I have to confess that it was quite a startling observation the first few times I saw it happen.

When my missus arrived in Singapore, Dave and I took her to the best roti prata place. We called over one of the women at the stall to take our order. As she stood beside our table, she turned her face to one side, spat into the gutter and continued to write down our order as if nothing had happened. Now, this was not the first impression I wanted my better half to get of the place. Ironically, though, it is the only time that someone has spat while taking our food order in all the time that we have been in Singapore. However, it is not an incident easily forgotten.

As I say, it is a cultural thing among the older generations and it will eventually die out. What is funny though, in a sick way, is how hip these people would be on the streets of Dagenham. Growing up in my home town, everyone seems to go through a compulsory phase of thinking that it is cool to spit. Thus, that little spitting gang of Singaporeans could fit in well with London's teenagers. They would just fall down in the ball-scratching department.

Yet despite our testicle touching, our teenage spitting, our chatty hairdressers and, more importantly, our tendency not to embrace the Singaporean lifestyle, there is still a discernible emulation of the West here. And it is the quirky Western obsessions that amaze me. I am proud to say that in my entire life, I have only ever stepped in one Hard Rock Cafe. It was in Sydney and I was there, ironically enough, because my partner had been asked to get a few shirts for her Singaporean friends. Singaporeans just cannot get enough of this kind of American merchandise. What is it all about? By all means, wear a product from a country that you have actually visited but I know of many Singaporeans who have never been to any of the Hard Rock or Planet Hollywood outlets but wear their T-shirts. In fact, night markets all over the island sell imitation shirts by the dozen. I could go to Bishan and buy a phoney Hard Rock Bangkok shirt, but why would I? Does the younger generation here have no pride in its culture at all? I see youngsters wearing branded shirts that have come from everywhere but Asia while an Asian-themed restaurant called Celebrities Asia closed down because the long-term interest just was not there.

However, it is Singapore's attachment to its colonial past that really baffles me. The average citizen takes pride in his independent nation and believes that the role of the British should now be consigned to the history books. I could not agree more. Nevertheless, the invisible touch of the former colonial power can still be felt everywhere.

Just take a perfunctory glance at the city's major place names. Walk around the business district; street and building names like Raffles, Cavenagh, Victoria, Stamford and Canning will pop up. All of these places have been named after pompous English imperialists. Taking this even further, Fort Canning Hill was known as Bukit Larangan, which means 'Forbidden Hill' in Malay, before Raffles arrived in 1819. The hill was a sacred site to the Malays, who buried one of their kings there. Then Singapore's first British

Resident William Farquhar arrived and said, 'Malays, we're in charge here so piss off. This place is not of any practical use to anyone so I'm going to stick a nice bungalow at the summit. That way, I'm near to the bus stops, the MRT and P-Mart department store. If you don't like it, I'll have you shot. Now fetch me a drink.' A fort subsequently replaced the bungalow in 1859 and had to be named. Some bright spark must have pointed out that Farquhar was such a funny sounding name that it could lead to American tourists pronouncing it Fort 'fucker' Park. Although, in truth, that might have been more appropriate. Instead, the fort was named after Viscount George Canning, govenor-general of India at the time. That is fair enough. However, unless I am very much mistaken, Singapore has been an independent nation since 1965 and these days Britain is struggling to retain the Falklands Islands' sheep population, so I am convinced that there would be little uproar in Westminster if Fort Canning Hill was renamed Bukit Larangan. It would not affect the tourist dollar and besides, Singapore is trying to build its own identity.

Building its own identity, however, will not come about if the country keeps naming everything after bloody Raffles. I mean, how many public sites, roads and buildings can be named after one man? And I would also like to state for the record that Raffles did not build Singapore at all. The migrants who flocked to Singapore in the nineteenth century built this country, not a man who spent less time on the island than my mate Scott.

Nevertheless, Singapore persists with maintaining links with its colonial past. If you are not convinced, go to either the Phoenix or Westin Stamford Hotels and order a taxi. There will be a porter on hand to hail the taxi on your behalf. Only this is no ordinary porter. This is an old Chinese guy dressed up to look like Phileas

Fogg on safari. He is togged out in the most embarrassing colonial costume. His polished brown shoes neatly complement his knee-high socks, which are invaluable leg protectors from all the reptiles and poisonous insects that hide in the vast undergrowth that is Somerset Road. His matching khaki shirt and shorts set ensures he does not get separated from his party of jungle explorers while his pith helmet not only keeps the spears of those tribal natives at bay but also guarantees that the poor man spends his entire working day looking a complete prat. I used to see the porter outside Phoenix Hotel every day on my way home from work and say hello. Of course, what I really wanted to say was 'Dr Livingstone, I presume?'

I have only picked on these two hotels because I have actually seen the extras from *Dad's Army* in action. I have been told that porters at some other major hotels have to wear similar uniforms. In fact, for all we know, there could be a string of uncles up and down the country standing outside a hotel right now, dressed like one of the country's old colonial masters. A rational explanation is quite beyond me. Surely it cannot possibly be in the money-driven name of tourism. When I stayed in Luxor, I was not greeted by porters dressed like Augustus, the Roman Emperor who conquered Cleopatra's Egypt. Having said this, I did spot people wearing silly costumes when I visited the Luxor Hotel in Las Vegas but this is a country that bought the wrong London Bridge.

If hotel management is so hell-bent on dressing up its staff, then it should at least allow them to wear their own period costumes. Why not, for example, allow the staff here to wear the *kebaya* or a sarong? At the very least, the uncles should be allowed to wear the shirt and blazer that the rest of the hotel staff wears to achieve consistency. Given the choice, I would rather wear a giant condom than a khaki suit once worn by a British aristocrat. I have got more in common with the condom.

As far as I am concerned, leave the West to the Westerners. After all, and I hope the MTV generation is paying attention here, they are so much better at being Western. So those Singaporeans who put ang mohs on such a bloody pedestal, stop it right now. Nothing would make me happier than to see Singaporeans dressing, talking, eating and drinking like Singaporeans. At this point, someone will say 'But there is no particular Singaporean identity for us to hang our coat on.' My response is: what the hell do you think I have been trying to say? Forget the colonial past, sidestep those bars full of pissed Australian tourists and turn away from the stars and stripes. Singapore only has an interesting future if it is a unique one and this will never come about as long as there are old Chinese porters dressed like Stamford Raffles on safari.

Chapter Fifteen

The only problem I have with Singapore's wonderful climate is that it makes me pee. Well, the humidity gives me an unquenchable thirst, which I try in vain to satisfy by drinking half of the country's Malaysian water supply. Recently, I needed to urinate so badly that I became cross-eyed and developed a walk that suggested I had one leg shorter than the other. Making my way to the public toilet, I noticed that an infuriating yellow 'do not enter' sign was blocking the doorway. I have a strong suspicion that these signs actually begin their life brilliant white but turn yellow over time as frustrated toilet-goers urinate over them.

Not easily deterred, I noticed that the cleaner had almost finished mopping the floor so I asked her if I could go in. She nodded and stepped outside to let me pass. Letting out one of those healthy 'aahs', I was in the middle of my private call of nature when I heard a swooshing sound. Taking a discreet look over my shoulder, I realised that the auntie was standing right behind me, mopping the floor without a care in the world. Thinking I was imagining things, I rubbed my eyes (with one hand, of course) and took a second look. To my horror, she was most certainly there, cleaning the floor just millimetres from my feet. It suddenly dawned on me that if I turned anything other than my head around, I could be arrested for gross public indecency. I was half tempted to whip around and cry 'What do you think of that then, auntie? You don't get many of those to a pound, do you?' But I strongly suspected that she might have giggled and mentioned something about already having *bee hoon* for breakfast.

This is not the first time that this has happened. Off the top of my head, I can recall three separate occasions when an auntie has been cleaning a public toilet while I have had the old willy out and none of them displayed the slightest hint of embarrassment. Yet I have never had such a strange encounter in a public toilet in England before. The closest I have ever come was when I went home for Scott's wedding last year. I was in the toilets in a club in Dagenham when I found myself in a conversation with a young bloke who inexplicably began and ended every sentence with the word 'fuck'.

It was most bizarre. I was washing my hands and chatting to a friend about my new job in Singapore. When I mentioned the word 'journalist', a voice said, 'Fucking hell, mate. You're a journalist, fuck. For which paper?'

Looking up, I saw a guy in his early twenties walking towards me, doing up his zip. He joined me at the sink.

'It's called the *Straits Times*, mate. It's the national paper in Singapore, mate.'

If it sounds like I was using the word 'mate' quite frequently, all I can say is strike up a conversation with a loud, drunk chap in an empty public toilet (my friend had disappeared pretty sharpish) and see what approach you would adopt.

'Fuck,' he continued, 'that's great, mate. Nice one. What do you write about then, like?'

'I cover local sports over there.'

'Fucking hell, mate. That's blinding that is, mate. So what the fuck are you doing in Dagenham?'

'I'm from Dagenham. I'm visiting my family.' I hoped that a shared socioeconomic background might impress the bloke, who seemed to have no intention of leaving or washing his hands for that matter.

'Ah, you're from Dagenham, fuck. Yeah, I live in Dagenham as well, mate. Fucking hell, small world, innit? So Singapore, lot of thieving over there like there is over here?' This was a loaded question and I had no idea what kind of answer would pacify him.

I said, 'Well, there's good and bad everywhere. I've got respect for both places. Anyway, I've got to go.' And I left him to his swearing.

In among all that nonsense, there was an obvious truth. I do sincerely respect both places. I love Singapore. For a country that is considered, again by Westerners who rarely come here, to be static and uniform, I still find it wonderfully varied. Where else in the world could you empty your bladder while an endearing old auntie, whom you have never seen before, stands over your shoulder?

This is the country where I can be sitting on my settee in my boxer shorts watching television, when Mr Eggy knocks on my door. He is a lovely old Chinese guy who walks along the corridors of my HDB block selling trays of eggs from a trolley. No matter how many eggs I already have, I make a habit of always buying a tray from him. Because as far as I am concerned, computers, the Internet and all those other geeky things will never replace the warmth of the personal touch. The same goes for the owners of the local mini-mart who always try to have a conversation with me using their smattering of English. Not only is it humbling because my knowledge of local languages is so inadequate but it unfailingly serves to remind me why I enjoy the company of the average Singaporean so much.

This was further brought home to me after a trip to the wonderful Sungei Buloh Nature Park. I went with Lawrence, who was returning to Canada shortly after and wanted to take in as many sights as possible. The park is set way back on Neo Tiew Crescent, which is in the middle of nowhere and dotted with just the odd industrial site and a few farms. I would thoroughly recommend the park to any Singaporean or tourist but would advise a couple of precautions. If you have a car, take the car. Alternatively, order a taxi or ensure that you leave the reserve by 7 p.m. to catch the last public bus of the day. Lawrence and I failed to do any of the above so we found ourselves stranded outside the closed park at 7:30 p.m., facing the prospect of an extremely long walk just to get to the main road because we had no loose change to call a taxi.

Having foolishly walked for most of the day on an empty stomach, we were left with only one rational alternative. We decided to hitchhike. It sounds crazy but at least it gives an indication of how utterly desperate we both were. A lorry approached and we both waved to the driver who, understandably, pulled over to the roadside with extreme caution. A Chinese guy in his mid-thirties warily leaned over and asked what we wanted. I put on my most sincere face and said, 'We're really sorry to bother you but we've just missed the last bus and the only way out of here now is to walk. We were just wondering if you wouldn't mind dropping us off at the main road.'

He thought about it for a few seconds, his mind obviously entertaining a number of doubts, before he finally agreed. We could not believe it. Lawrence sat in the front with the guy and I sat in the back. Coming out onto the main road, I realised that the guy was going even further and intended to drop us off right outside Kranji MRT station. Now he was going way beyond the call of duty. There was a dusky cool breeze blowing and as we travelled along one of the more rural parts of the island, I vividly recall watching Lawrence through the window having an animated conversation with our Singaporean Samaritan and I remember feeling lucky to be here.

The guy said he ran a guppy breeding farm. Well, if a guppy breeder who once gave a lift to two ang mohs ever reads this, can I just say that you are a thoroughly decent human being. But then so are the majority of Singaporeans that I have come to know. Whether they be the eccentric characters in my HDB block, the fans of S-League football or the hundreds of schoolchildren that I have been fortunate enough to teach, they have all been honest, hardworking people.

But I wonder how things will be for Singapore in future. All the things I love about Singapore are evolving in the name of efficiency and productivity. Just like in England, the little man is mercilessly being crushed.

Take hawker centres. My uncle's café in London eventually succumbed to the larger supermarket chains with their everything-under-one-roof concept. And there is nothing to suggest that hawker centres will not go the same way. Sanitised, expensive food courts are already in the process of replacing their grimy predecessors but at what cost? These food courts are ripping the soul out of what is a fundamental component of Singapore's food culture. Step into any food court and you will detect the lack of atmosphere. The whole place is subdued, conservative and, dare I say it, boring. For me, at least, a meal in a hawker centre is an adventure. It is land of a thousand faces. Loud, rumbustious stall owners try to entice you to their particular delicacy while groups of diners at a hundred tables talk animatedly. Old timers sit and watch the world go by while nursing a Tiger beer as dozens of school kids rush in to grab their lunch. That is an eating experience. But going to a food court, with its fluorescent lighting, is about as exciting as a trip to the dentist.

To me, that is just one of the signs of the kiasu times. The money-driven people have no time for the hawker centre. They eat on the run and get back to the office to add a few more cents to their annual bonus. That is what the nation's government wants its people to do. A good citizen is a productive citizen. Whether it is the auntie mopping the floor while I am in the toilet or the stock trader in Shenton Way, they must all contribute to the country's primary goal of bringing in the green. A nonproductive Singaporean is a bad Singaporean. Retraining is the order of the day. We must keep learning, whether we are five or sixty-five, so we can continue to raise productivity and the nation's coffers. Then, and only then, can the majority afford the car, the condo, the maid and the country club and be just like everybody else.

But wait a minute. This twenty-first-century 'Brave New World' concept has one major flaw. This production line could well run out of producers. With young executives hell-bent in turning their three months bonus into a 3.5 months bonus, where is the sex? There may be just enough time for a quick shag with one's fellow executive colleague (clever people cannot sleep with stupid people) before collapsing into bed. But as for having babies, well, one or two is all the maid can realistically cope with. A third baby might put the condo back a couple of years and we cannot have that now, can we?

This unquestionably leads to falling birth rates and Singaporeans are now failing in their civic duties to bolster the nation's labour forces. Hence, the government has introduced financial incentives to encourage couples to have that third child. Many Singaporeans, thankfully, have been appalled by this course of action. Producing a life should not be decided by one or two token subsidies but one or two letter writers to the *Straits Times* have expressed gratitude to the government for reducing the financial load of having a third child and they now consider it a viable option.

Since when did a human life evolve into a consumer durable? I remember watching the annual budgets when I was a kid and my mother being concerned by the tax increases levied on cigarettes. If they had not been raised too much, she would send me out to buy a packet. She kicked the habit a couple of years ago, I am proud to say. Well, in Singapore, there are village idiots acting in a similar fashion with babies. I can imagine them at home watching the prime minister's speech and saying 'Ooh, that latest discount on a third child is a good deal. We should get one now before the special offer ends.' It will end if and when the birth rate begins to rise again and there will then be a special offer introduced for those who stop at having one or two children. It is ironic really because pessimists once painted a miserable Orwellian future for Singapore. I believe Huxley's *Brave New World* is now much closer to the mark – a place where everyone aspires to be the same thing: a greedy, selfish arsehole.

And if this world is to become a reality, what will happen to the locals that I really do admire? There will be no place in a condo for the likes of Mr Eggy, the aunties in my mini-mart or Saudita, my legendary old landlady. The very people who helped build this country will be left by the wayside and all the spiel in the world about 'retraining' will not change that. Wonderful but crazy characters around my HDB block like Vidal Sassoon and bra lady will have no role to play in the New Economy. And when that tragic day finally comes and the geeks and the greedy take over completely, I like to think that I will be sitting in a coffee shop with Mr Kong, laughing at one of his eccentric reminiscences.

This, however, is all in the future. It might yet be avoided if the government declares kiasuism to be a disease of the mind, which requires a spell in a mental institute.

Right now, though, Singapore remains a great place to be. Despite spending most of my life on the outskirts of a sprawling, unpredictable city like London, Singapore is still a colourful, vibrant metropolis that is full of variety if you go looking for it.

Where else in the world would you encounter a landlady who has a penchant for preparing food with her bared breasts bouncing all over the kitchen? Or adorable kids not only refer to a penis as a cuckoo bird but also call you one for good measure? This is a country where its cab drivers are either demanding your life story or warning you of the perils of organ stealing government hospitals. The island's most feared group of people are the hordes of aunties who can carry half a supermarket in two plastic bags, knock out an entire bus queue with one shoulder, barge and be on call to drown any unwanted rats with their bare hands. Believe me, no two days are the same in Singapore.

My partner teaches at a pre-school that is tucked away in a little rural haven. After a stressful morning of chasing rich kids around a classroom, my girlfriend retired to the lavatory to be alone with her thoughts, plan her afternoon's activities and, most importantly, empty her bladder. Sitting on the throne, she heard a gentle splashing sound, which was somewhat startling because she had not actually started doing anything yet. Slowly, she got up and turned around to find Singapore's biggest frog gamely attempting the breaststroke. Her initial scream terrified the entire school and almost broke Freddie the Frog's concentration. However, the shock was short-lived. She quickly regained her senses, washed her hands and gently picked up the frog and released it into the garden. She said he looked grateful but muttered something about having his 'bloody training schedule messed up for the amphibian Olympics'.

Her bravery left me speechless. Had the same incident occurred to me then, I guarantee that Tanglin Road would have been greeted by the sight of a lanky Caucasian, waddling like a penguin with his underpants round his ankles, waving his tackle about and shouting, 'There's a fucking frog up my arse!'

I cannot deny it. My urban working-class upbringing has left me totally unprepared for the trials and tribulations of living in a tropical Asian country and it is wonderful. Every incident in Singapore is a brand new experience that I am wholly unequipped for. And the best part is, I know another one will come along tomorrow.

Of course, the time will come when I will return to England to the faint strains of my mother's voice crying 'Where the hell are my grandchildren?' And eventually, in the dim and distant future, I will find myself in an English pub having yet another futile argument over the quality of life. Only this time, I will lean across the table, wink knowingly and whisper, 'You know, you ain't never lived until you've had a huge frog swimming laps in your toilet bowl.' My friends will fall silent and I will sit back contentedly, with a boyish grin slapped across my face. That, in a nutshell, is why I would rather be here now.

About the Author

Neil Humphreys grew up in the working-class town of Dagenham, Essex, where he survived one of the worst comprehensive school educations in Britain and two muggings. In 1993, he escaped to the University of Manchester and argued his way to a First Class Honours degree in history. After graduating in 1996, however, he soon realised that the ability to distinguish Nazism from Fascism was less popular in Dagenham than the ability to drink large quantities of alcohol. Therefore, he decided to travel.

Singapore was suggested. He immediately agreed and bought a book on China to discover which province the city was in. After getting by as an English teacher with a strong cockney accent for two years, he switched to journalism. In 2001, *Notes from an Even Smaller Island* was released in Singapore and became an immediate best-seller. The book has since travelled across South-east Asia, Australia and Britain. In 2003, the best-selling sequel *Scribbles from the Same Island* was published. When he is not writing, he likes to spend his time in Singapore not getting mugged.